ELECTRONIC MAIL

A Revolution in Business Communications

by
Stephen Connell
and Ian A. Galbraith

Knowledge Industry Publications, Inc.

Office Productivity Series

Electronic Mail: A Revolution in Business Communications

Library of Congress Cataloging in Publication Data

Connell, Stephen.
    Electronic mail.

    (Office productivity series)
    Includes index.
    1. Electronic mail systems.   2. Communication in
management.   I. Galbraith, Ian A.   II. Title.
III. Series.
HE6239.E54C66   384.1'4   82-44
ISBN 0-86729-015-3   AACR2
ISBN 0-86729-016-1 (pbk.)

First edition copyright © 1980 by Mackintosh International, Mackintosh House, Napier Road, Luton,
England LU1 1RG, and Communications Studies and Planning Ltd., Circus House, 21 Titchfield
Street, London, England W1P 7FD.

Additional material copyright © 1982 by Knowledge Industry Publications, Inc., 701 Westchester
Avenue, White Plains, New York 10604.

Printed in the United States of America.

10   9   8   7   6   5   4   3   2   1

Table of Contents

List of Tables and Figures

Preface

The concept of electronic mail is rapidly gaining acceptance in the business community as an efficient, cost-effective communications alternative. Faced with declining mail service, escalating costs and an increasing emphasis on time as a precious business commodity, more and more organizations are investigating electronic mail as a steppingstone to improved office productivity. Not only existing services like telex and facsimile, but such newer technologies as communicating word processors or packet-switched networks, can be the building blocks of an electronic mail system.

Indeed, electronic mail has the potential to revolutionize business communications. However, few organizations have the information needed to plan for its adoption, or even to judge its potential in the context of their daily operations. This book is intended to fill that information vacuum. It is the product of a major study, "Electronic Mail in the USA and Western Europe," undertaken by Mackintosh Consultants and Communications Studies and Planning Ltd. Initiated in 1977 and completed in 1980, the study collected data on the need for, and potential of, electronic mail at organizations throughout North America and Europe.

Material from the study was then supplemented with information on the current technology and services for electronic mail, including such new offerings as the U.S. Postal Service's controversial E-COM, or the international facsimile service, INTELPOST.

This book is designed to assist organizational managers who wonder how electronic systems can improve intra-office and external mail services. The first three chapters orient readers who may not be familiar with the concepts and technology of telecommunications, computing and electronic mail. Chapter 1 discusses the basic components of an electronic mail system and defines a number of technological terms. An analysis of current mail use, user needs and desirable system features is presented in Chapter 2. A detailed description of the various technological elements of electronic mail systems (e.g., communications equipment, transmission systems, etc.) is provided in Chapter 3.

Following this technical groundwork, Chapter 4 goes on to examine the arguments for adopting electronic mail, in terms of its cost-effectiveness and efficiency. Chapter 5 offers an overview of electronic mail system design, with case studies of seven companies that have such systems in place. Chapter 6 covers the step-by-step process for designing electronic mail systems in individual organizations.

Worldwide policy and regulation issues and their impact on electronic mail are discussed in Chapter 7. Chapter 8 examines the prospects for transmission services in America and Europe, reviewing current and proposed offerings. The difficult questions of electronic mail's acceptance and potential growth are dealt with in Chapter 9.

Finally, two appendixes provide valuable information on electronic mail suppliers: Appendix A gives brief profiles of major equipment manufacturers and transmission services and Appendix B lists the names and addresses of representative suppliers.

Because the technology of electronic mail is changing rapidly, as new equipment and services are introduced, readers cannot find in any one volume all the information needed to make intelligent choices. But it is hoped that by laying out a framework for understanding electronic mail, this report will equip managers to gather and evaluate all the information required to make the best decision for their own particular organizations.

* * * * * * * *

Mackintosh Consultants, Ltd. is a leading research and management consultant firm specializing in the worldwide electronics sector. It has conducted numerous international studies on the impact of electronics technology on the office equipment market and office environment.

Communications Studies and Planning Ltd. (CS&P) is an international professional service organization specializing in communications, telecommunications and information technology. CS&P has planned communications/information systems and developed new applications for computer and communications technologies for clients throughout Europe.

Section I: User Needs and System Concepts

- ✔ **Why Electronic Mail Is Timely**

- ✔ **An Electronic Mail Scenario**

- ✔ **Types of Terminal Equipment**

- ✔ **Types of Transmission Systems**

- ✔ **Determining the Needs of Users**

- ✔ **Determining Desirable Features for Electronic Mail Systems**

- ✔ **The Microelectronics Revolution**

- ✔ **Printing, Imaging, Display and Other Techniques**

- ✔ **Cost and Performance Projections for Terminals**

- ✔ **Cost and Performance Projections for Transmission Services**

1

An Overview of Electronic Mail

What is electronic mail? Briefly, it is any one of a number of ways to send written or printed information by electronic means. There is scarcely an organization that does not send or receive *some* messages electronically today, but typically these messages account for a minute proportion of total communications traffic. We are in the midst of a proliferation of electronic communication systems that is so pervasive, however, that it cannot help but affect your own organization. Thus, the implications of electronic mail are real and immediate. They need to be confronted by every organization involved in communications, from the legal practice that consists only of a lawyer and secretary to the multibillion dollar corporation that employs hundreds of thousands of people and that operates its own communications network around the world.

This guide is intended to help you understand better the nature of electronic mail, to assess its implications, and to plan for them. As far-reaching as the implications of electronic mail may be, it is important to stress a point that will become clearer in the course of this book, namely, that electronic mail is not for everybody today.

Electronic mail makes the most sense for the organization that needs rapid communication among departments in different sites. Such an organization can invest in the equipment for electronic mail without worrying about whether the equipment is compatible with that of its customers or suppliers. Such an organization is also spending enough money on conventional postal service, courier service or data communications for its own internal uses, to warrant looking at a comprehensive, organization-wide electronic mail system.

Other applications of electronic mail are important as well, such as communication with customers, or the efficient handling of messages among a large number of people in a single location. But the company that must communicate with its own branches in different locations will find it easiest to justify an investment in electronic message systems.

WHY ELECTRONIC MAIL IS TIMELY

The decade of the 1980s has already seen striking progress in both the technology of electronic mail and in the development of electronic mail networks. Some recent developments include:

- Announcement of low-cost word processors with "communications capability," which simply means that they can send messages to similar machines—suppliers include such firms as Xerox, IBM, Wang, Philips and Digital Equipment Corp.;

- Announcement of specifications for local area networks (LANS) operating within a single establishment; these local networks use coaxial cable or optical fibers to connect different pieces of equipment, thus facilitating intra-organizational messages. Ethernet, a joint specification from Xerox, Digital Equipment Corp. and Intel, and WangNet, a competing offering from Wang, are two of the best known such systems;

- Inauguration of Intelpost, an international facsimile message service coordinated by the postal and telecommunications authorities of the U.K., U.S., Canada and European countries;

- Awarding of a contract for terminals for E-COM, a controversial U.S. Postal Service service that is intended to combine electronic communication with physical delivery of a sealed letter. Bulk mail users send messages from their computers to computers at 25 post office centers, which deliver the messages to addressees in two business days;

- Development of a European standard, called Teletex, for much-improved telex service and for combined text-and-graphics terminals; West Germany is the first country to implement the new class of equipment.

All these developments come at a time when the cost of traditional postal service, and other paper-based message systems, continues to increase. At the same time, progress in microelectronics and telecommunications is bringing down the cost of the terminals and transmission circuits that are the building blocks of electronic mail. While much of the technology for electronic mail is here now, however, its economics are not always well understood. And equally important, how this technology can be adapted to existing ways of working, and to existing organizational structures, is a serious question mark.

Before we attempt to analyze these issues, it is essential to define electronic mail more fully. This chapter first provides an electronic mail scenario, then introduces the basic technical components of the service and defines a number of terms. (The technological discussion presented in this chapter assumes no prior knowledge of electronic mail and telecommunications. Later chapters will examine the technology in more detail.)

AN ELECTRONIC MAIL SCENARIO

The Electronic Letter Arrives

John Andrews is a regional accounts manager for the XYZ Manufacturing Corp. Arriving at work in the morning, he finds on his desk a request (sent electronically) from one of his best customers for price and availability quotations on XYZ's latest models. The customer needs this by 1:30 p.m., in advance of a senior management meeting. (Figure 1.1 outlines the events that follow.)

Figure 1.1 Outline of an Electronic Mail Scenario

Overnight	Electronic letter arrives: request for bid
10:30 a.m.	Reply is dictated
11:00 a.m.	Draft is typed
11:20 a.m.	Final revisions completed
11:22 a.m.	Editing completed on word processor
11:23 a.m.	Reply sent and received electronically
11:24 a.m.	Copy sent electronically to assistant
11:25 a.m.	Copies sent electronically to central files and printed for personal files

By 10:30 a.m. John has dictated a letter to his secretary containing the necessary information. By 11:00 a.m. the first draft has been typed, and John makes a few small corrections. By 11:20 a.m. he has read the revised copy and approved it for mailing. He gives the following instructions to his secretary: "Send the letter, and make sure it arrives at the customer's office by 1:30 p.m.; send copies of the correspondence to the national accounts manager [John Andrews' supervisor at headquarters] to arrive by tomorrow, and to the assistant manager, immediately, for him to follow up on in the morning. Also, file the correspondence with copies to the central files."

Sending the Response Electronically

To do this, the secretary sits down in front of her word processor, which consists of a keyboard and a display that looks like a small TV screen.

The final draft of the letter is still being held in the electronic memory of the word processor. Typing an index number displays the letter on the screen. A single push-button automatically inserts an electronic picture of the company's letterhead. The secretary types codes for "immediate delivery" and "reply," and with two single-word commands, designates the address on the inside heading of the letter to the system. She then pushes the red button on the processor marked "send." The word processor is directly connected to the telephone system, and contains an automatic dialer. Within seconds of pushing the send button, the word processor has dialed-up a central computer which is the entry-point for an electronic mail network and has sent the letter, along with the picture of the letterhead, and the information about the address. Within a few seconds the central computer has replied with an answer-back code, a special abbreviation of the name of the company to which the message was sent (which allows checking that the address had been correctly typed), along with the words "message received." The message has been delivered.

Delivering Copies Electronically to Associates

The customer's original letter is also in the electronic memory of the processor. The secretary extracts this, and, with a couple of commands, "attaches" it as a second "page" of the letter. Preceding the letters she inserts a note: "FYI. Will inform you of outcome tomorrow p.m. — John." She then designates "overnight delivery" and "no reply," pulls the national manager's address out of a memory in the word processor that contains addresses and telephone numbers, and pushes the send button.

The secretary types a new memo to the assistant manager, erasing the one to the national manager: "Please follow this up tomorrow a.m. and report back to me by noon — John." She then types in the assistant manager's room number and pushes the send button. The system recognizes this as an internal number, and dials it on the internal telephone exchange. Within a couple of seconds, there is an acknowledgement from the word processor at the assistant's office.

Filing the Correspondence Electronically

Now for the filing. One command deletes the memo. The secretary types in the address of the central files, hits the send button, and receives acknowledgement. Since John likes to keep his files on paper, the secretary punches the address of the printer that is shared by all the offices nearby. She hits the send button, receives acknowledgement and walks down the corridor. She picks up the letters from the printer, files them in her boss's filing cabinet and returns to her desk. It's now 11:25 a.m.

In five minutes, and in leaving her desk only once, John's secretary has fulfilled all of his instructions: she has ensured delivery of the letter to the customer, sent copies to John's boss and subordinate and filed them twice; once electronically in the master file, and once on paper in his personal file.

EMERGENCE OF ELECTRONIC MAIL AS A VIABLE INDUSTRY

If the above scenario sounds futuristic, keep this in mind:

- Everything described could easily be accomplished with current technology.

- The chances are that within a few years the word processing system described will cost no more than an average word processor sold today. In fact, the price of some models could be closer to that of a current office typewriter.

- The cost of delivery, while impossible to predict because of regulation, should in no case cost more than a one-minute phone call. Assuming that government policy-makers allow it, and the telephone companies or government-owned telephone administrations (PTTs) in the various countries offer it, overnight delivery could be even cheaper, and overseas, overnight delivery could cost less than an airmail stamp.

It is also important to keep in mind the savings in direct labor, in materials like paper and envelopes, in printing, copying, inventory and all of the indirect labor costs. Notice, too, how easily electronic mail combines with other advances in office equipment and organization, such as central electronic filing.

The next section describes technologies involved in electronic mail, reviewing basic telecommunications concepts and types of office equipment.

ELEMENTS OF ELECTRONIC MAIL SYSTEMS

Conceptually, any electronic mail system consists of two elements: 1) the terminal and 2) the transmission system. A third element, or function, consists of a place for storing and forwarding messages—this place can be a computer that is part of the transmission network, or it can be within one of the terminals.

The terminal is the piece of equipment normally located on the user's premises. Its job is to convert the message to an electronic code suitable for transmission, and conversely, to receive a code and convert it to a readable form. The transmission system takes the code given it by the originating terminal and delivers it to the destination terminal.* Transmission systems are most often operated by a PTT or telephone company.

The discussion that follows describes the most common types of terminals and transmission systems.

TYPES OF TERMINAL EQUIPMENT

The easiest way to distinguish between different kinds of terminal equipment is by the kinds of information they handle. The two most important types of terminals are *text* and *facsimile,* and the difference between them is central to an understanding of electronic mail.

Imagine having to send a written message by means of an electronic signal. Conceptually there are at least two ways you can do it. One way would be to send a picture of it, much as a television signal is sent. This is, broadly speaking, what facsimile terminals do and in practice they work very much like remote photocopying machines. The other way would be to translate the message, letter by letter, according to some sort of conventional code, say Morse code. This is what text terminals do, though of course they don't use Morse code but one that is more suited to machine transmission. In practice text terminals work very much like an electronic typewriter.

Let's look at the differences more closely.

How Facsimile Terminals Work

An ideal facsimile terminal would produce a perfect copy by transmitting every point on the page it is reproducing separately to the output terminal. However, this is impossible since there are an infinite number of these points. Therefore, all facsimile terminals must make some compromise between the amount of information they use to represent the copy and the quality of its

---

*This is a broader definition than commonly used by telecommunications engineers, who distinguish transmission from switching and local distribution. For our purposes, however, it is sufficient to lump them together as "transmission."

reproduction; the more information, the smaller the minimum point and the better the resolution.

Analog Facsimile Terminals

Facsimile terminals work by scanning line by line across a page and measuring its reflectivity. High reflectivity indicates white, and low reflectivity indicates black. Sometimes each line of information is transmitted continuously, so that the signal produced is a wave form, with high amplitude corresponding to white areas, low amplitude to black areas, and the duration of each being the time it took to scan the white and black areas. This is called *analog* representation. A device holding a piece of paper the same size as the original document and a stylus moving across the new page on the same line and at the same rate as the original scanner are necessary to reproduce the image on the other end. If the ink from the stylus is controlled by the signal, so that high amplitude stops it and low amplitude allows it to flow, the output terminal will faithfully reproduce the original, limited only by the number of scanning lines, noise or interference in the signal, and the precision of the devices. (See Figure 1.2.)

Digital Facsimile Terminals

There is another way to represent the light and dark areas seen by the scanner. Instead of sending a continuous wave, the terminal can sample it at discrete points in time. For example, the terminal can look at the signal produced by the scanner 4800 times a second, and at each point decide whether the scanner is on a dark area or on a light one. For transmission (in its simplest form) if the area is light, the device sends a pulse down the line; if it's dark, it sends nothing. This is called *digital* representation. Digital representation has discrete values: in this case two, which can be represented by a 0 for when there is no pulse in a time period, and 1 for when there is a pulse in the time period. To reproduce the signal a device very much like the analog one is used, except that it is controlled by pulses—one every 1/4800 of a second—instead of a wave form. If it doesn't receive a pulse in an interval, it allows the stylus to write a tiny dot—if it does receive a pulse, it stops the stylus from writing.* Note that if the dots are small enough, it will be imposssible to distinguish them unless examined very closely.

---

*Of course, this explanation is oversimplified. Advanced digital systems do not send out a pulse for every picture element, but instead use "data compression" techniques. For example, a machine might send out a code that indicates only transitions: e.g., 20 black elements, 1000 white elements, etc. However, it would still need to do a digital sampling of each element, and the code would also still be digital.

It turns out that modern transmission and processing systems are better suited to digital signals than they are to analog ones. As we will see, digital facsimile terminals allow faster transmission than their analog competitors.

Figure 1.2 Analog and Digital Facsimile Representation

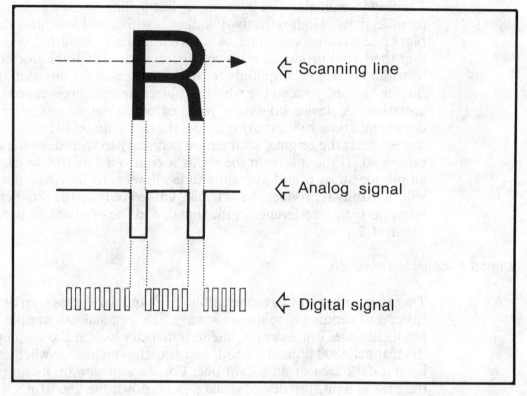

$\Leftarrow$ Scanning line

$\Leftarrow$ Analog signal

$\Leftarrow$ Digital signal

How Text Terminals Work

The other way to send a written message electronically is to encode each letter in the message, rather as an old-fashioned telegrapher would using Morse code. This is known as text representation. For machine purposes, it is more convenient to make each element of the code of the same duration, instead of the variable duration of Morse code's dots and dashes. Each letter is represented by the same number of elements, eight, which comprise time-slots where a pulse is either present or not—corresponding to the "zero" or "one" bits of binary code. Note then that the text representations are inherently digital in that the values are always discrete. (Figure 1.3 shows part of the code used by telex terminals.)

Figure 1.3 Code Used to Represent Alphabet* for Telex Terminals

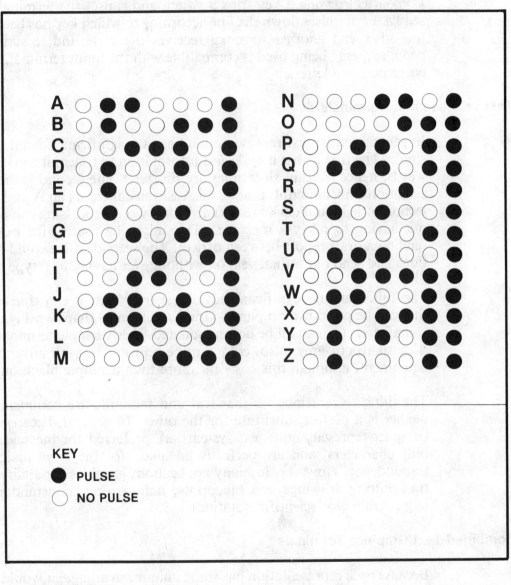

KEY
● PULSE
○ NO PULSE

*International Alphabet Number 2.

Creation of a text representation is simple: the most common input device is a keyboard. Pressing a key trips a switch and causes the terminal's circuits to send a set of pulses down the line according to which key has been pressed. At the other end another terminal receives the code and, assuming that the coding scheme being used is compatible with the input terminal, produces the corresponding letter.

Text vs. Facsimile Terminals

In general terms, text representation has two significant advantages over facsimile. The first is that it takes *less* information to transmit a given number of words, hence transmission times are shorter.* The second is that text representation is meaningful; that is, an A is transmitted as an A and not as a collection of light and dark areas. Therefore, word processing can be done without having to rekey a message. (This might be useful, for example, when sending a draft report between offices. The second office could make corrections and send out a final version without ever having to retype the original.)

Facsimile has one significant advantage over text: it can transmit anything that can be put down on paper. Graphs, diagrams, handwriting, non-Roman characters, etc., can all be accommodated. Fairly simple terminals can reproduce shades of grey; also, color can be reproduced with advanced facsimile equipment, although this costs far more than a simple black on white unit.

The thing to remember is that text and facsimile are complementary since neither is a perfect substitute for the other. In general, because of its more compact representation, text systems are preferred for messages containing only characters, and are perfectly adequate for the large majority of correspondence. However, in many applications graphics capability is essential: transmitting drawings and blueprints, handwriting, nonstandard typefaces (e.g., Arabic, or scientific notation).

Combined Text/Graphics Terminals

Because each representation has some unique advantage, it would be useful to have one terminal capable of handling both forms of reproduction. As it turns out, the technical obstacles to combining text and graphics are no longer overwhelming when the new technology of microelectronics is fully applied to

---

*It is easy to see why. Each letter, which in text form can be represented by eight bits, must take dozens of bits to represent in facsimile. Moreover, facsimile terminals have to send information not only about the letters, but also about blank areas.

the problem and the graphics are digitally represented. Thus, by the mid-1980s equipment manufacturers will be marketing combined text/graphics terminals.

TYPES OF TRANSMISSION SYSTEMS

The next element of an electronic mail system to consider is the transmission system. Here, as with terminal equipment, a number of different options are possible: telephone networks, telex and data networks. We will look at each in turn.

The Public Telephone Network

Telephones are quite capable of sending electronic mail traffic: transmission times range from about six minutes per page for primitive analog facsimile machines, to a few seconds for a page of text. There are also a number of advantages to using the telephone network. Essentially every potential addressee possesses a telephone, and, except for a couple of periods during the day, there is plenty of capacity in the telephone network for electronic mail traffic. Note, for example, the utilization curve for the trunk-telephone network in the Federal Republic of Germany which is typical of many countries. (See Figure 1.4.) Outside the business day it is never more than 60% utilized, with close to 0% usage between midnight and 6 a.m. Even in the middle of the day, during lunch hour, utilization falls almost to 50%.

Advantages and Disadvantages of the Telephone Network

This low average utilization means that, in theory, there is plenty of room for electronic mail in addition to voice traffic; especially since in most cases overnight delivery or an hour or two delay is perfectly acceptable for mail service. The problem, of course, is to be able to take advantage of these service lulls to send a message, since lulls occur exactly because they are the least convenient times for use. What is needed is a system with the ability to store a message in memory of some sort, and forward it automatically at the appropriate time.

This "store-and-forward" capability can be built into a terminal by providing it with a memory and an automatic dialing/answering machine. Alternatively the memory could be built into the transmission network itself. Thus the network would be able to transmit electronic mail messages whenever there was spare capacity available, minimizing the need for sophisticated terminals. (Store-and-forward techniques are further discussed in Chapter 3.)

Figure 1.4 Utilization of Trunk Telephone Network in the Federal Republic of Germany by Time of Day

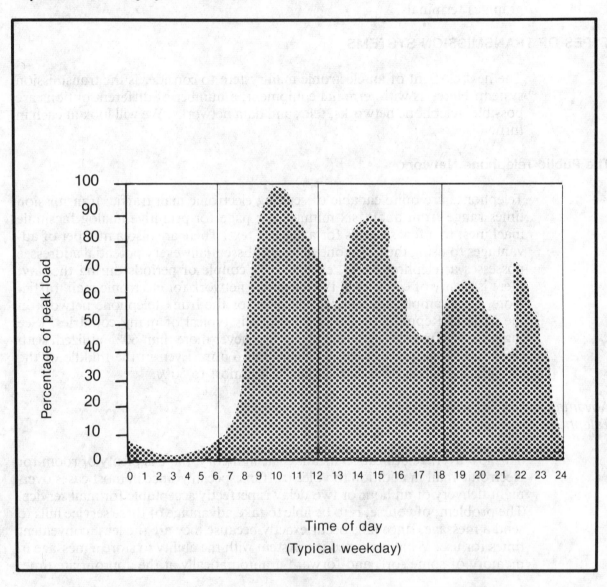

Time of day

(Typical weekday)

Source: Mackintosh International and Communication Studies and Planning Ltd., 1978.

The major disadvantages of the public telephone network result from the fact that it and its rate structure were not designed specifically for electronic mail. For example, most long-distance calls have a minimum charging period of one minute or longer. This is well suited to conversations but may seriously increase the cost of electronic mail usage where transmission may only require five or 10 seconds. Similarly, store-and-forward, so useful for electronic mail, is not provided in normal telephone systems because it is useless for conversations. However, the technology of digital voice store-and-forward is being developed for prerecorded voice message services, and trial services are likely to be introduced in many countries during the 1980s. One such service currently offered in the United States is Voicemail, a service of Televoice International in Santa Clara, CA.

As demand for electronic mail services becomes stronger in the early 1980s, it will be in the interest of telephone companies and administrations to offer rate structures and services such as store-and-forward for electronic mail. This is because electronic mail offers them a new source of revenue at relatively little additional cost in terms of new telephone exchanges or lines. We will examine different services further in Chapter 8, but it is important to keep in mind that the primary means of transmission for electronic mail will be the public telephone network, albeit somewhat modified.

Other Transmission Systems for Electronic Mail

The Use of the Telex Network

Telex's major advantage over other forms of electronic mail is that it already exists and has achieved widespread acceptance. However, telex is limited to upper case text with poor print quality, offers only a very slow transmission rate, and in most countries provides no store-and-forward capability in the network for national traffic. As such, it will be increasingly at a competitive disadvantage to electronic mail systems based on the telephone network or other transmission systems. In addition, in many countries the telex network is highly congested, resulting in a high proportion of rejected calls.

There is, however, some room for improvement in the telex service: transmission speeds can be increased, terminals can be improved and store-and-forward facilities can be provided, and this may offset some of the advantages of other electronic mail systems. But the rate at which this improvement can be accomplished is limited by the large commitment to existing telex network equipment with its very restricted capabilities.

Other electronic mail systems are likely to offer substantial advantages over telex for many users by the 1980s: among which are better print quality, superior service and lower costs.

The Use of Leased Lines

Many companies currently lease private lines from carriers between locations where they have a great deal of traffic. Often these are used for both data and voice communication. Electronic mail offers an extremely cost-effective means to utilize any excess capacity in these lines.

The Use of Data Networks

There are already networks in existence which were specifically designed to carry data traffic in digital form. But because various data users have different needs, these networks are not all the same.

One kind of network sends the data in packets (a set number of characters) from which is derived the name *packet-switched network*. In addition to data, each packet contains the address of the destination terminal; when more data than can fit in one packet must be sent, several are used. Each packet travels through the network independently and may follow different routes.

A similar kind of network is called *message-switched* which differs only in that the whole message is sent together, and may not be broken up into several units (as is necessary in packet-switched networks when a message is longer than the fixed size of a packet). The third major form of data network is called *circuit-switched* and uses end-to-end connections in much the same way as the telephone network.

Packet- and message-switched networks obtain an advantage from the fact that a line does not have to be clear at the time a message is sent, or held open during pauses. Thus, more users can share the same set of transmission lines, with a computer at every node in the network looking at the address of each packet or message, and sending it on to the next stage by fitting it into gaps. However, if very large amounts of data are to be sent quickly, the overhead associated with a computer having to look at each packet and decide where it should be routed becomes more expensive than the cost of setting up and holding an end-to-end connection. (Such computer costs are coming down quickly, however.)

Neither packet-switched nor circuit-switched data networks are often very cost-effective for electronic mail. Packet-switched networks are generally set up for interactive computer users, and designed, therefore, so that packets travel through them very quickly. Mail generally does not need this speed, although the speed is certainly not a disadvantage—it should be possible to arrange traffic so that interactive communication and urgent one-way messages take priority on packet-switched networks, with less important messages being transmitted in slack periods.

Circuit-switched lines, on the other hand, are expensive to set up for the relatively little data which the average electronic mail volume represents (this will be examined more closely in Chapter 2). However, for some applications, for example where there are large numbers of facsimile messages between locations, or where there is a mixture of computer and electronic mail traffic, these systems may be quite cost-effective. Message-switched systems are, by and large, the most useful for electronic mail, but are not widely available because they are more expensive to build than packet-switched systems.

The Use of Hybrid Networks

Hybrid networks combine electronic transmission with physical transmission. The best example is the ordinary telegram, where the message is hand-delivered to the addressee from a local terminal. A similar service is the Mailgram service operated by Western Union and the Postal Service in the United States, where electronically transmitted messages are printed near the destination post office and mailed for next day delivery.

Hybrid networks offer an important service for the wider acceptance of electronic mail in that they make it possible for users to reach addressees who do not own their own terminals, and vice versa. While more cumbersome and expensive to use than a direct system, a hybrid system can still offer substantial service advantages compared to standard post, along with cost advantages over courier services.

SUMMARY

This chapter has introduced some of the basic concepts of electronic mail. We have seen some of the variation possible in the functional elements of an electronic mail system: terminals and transmission systems. A key concept is the difference between facsimile and text representation: facsimile is analogous to a television picture, and requires a great deal of information to represent; text is a meaningful code, and requires much less information, but is able to represent only those characters in the character set. Among transmission systems, we have noted that a number of options are available, from the telephone network to data networks or hybrid systems. An important concept here, and one to which we will return, is that of store-and-forward capability.

2

How Organizations Use the Mail

For electronic mail, where substantial investment may be required to perform a function generally served by a postage stamp, a careful examination of applications and costs is essential. In later chapters we will be looking carefully at costs; here we examine applications. We start by describing how medium to large organizations use the mail, and go on to summarize their perceptions of these services—their satisfactions and complaints—and derive from these desirable features for electronic mail systems.

The data presented in this chapter are based on an extensive survey carried out by Mackintosh Consultants and Communications Studies and Planning Ltd. This survey produced a massive data base including:

- Measurement of the total mail flowing into 130 establishments;

- 13,000 responses to special questionnaires, which collected very detailed data about individual mail items;

- 1700 telephone interviews;

- 215 in-depth, personal interviews.

Of course, information about typical patterns of usage is much less useful for detailed planning in individual organizations than specific local data, and in Chapter 6 we will discuss how organizations can survey their own needs. In the meantime, as this discussion proceeds, it is useful to think about:

- How much your organization knows about its own pattern of use of mail facilities and its own requirements;

- The extent to which your organization is typical.

Keep in mind that, for the purposes of defining a statistical sample, we looked at the following kinds of organizations:

- Manufacturing establishments with more than 50 employees;

- Government, transport, communications, retail and wholesale distribution establishments with more than 10 employees;

- Financial, business, and professional service establishments of all sizes.*

DETERMINING THE NEEDS OF USERS

The question "How do organizations use the mail?" can be broken down into three subsidiary questions:

- How much mail do they send?

- What means do they use (and why)?

- What do they send?

The question "How much do they send?" gives us some idea of the level of investment required in individual companies, and the potential in each for electronic mail services. "What means do they use?" indicates the needs for various types of services, and the premiums users place on them. The last question, "What do they send?" tells us about some features that are useful, or even essential, for wide acceptance of electronic mail, and about the costs and relative strengths of rival electronic systems.

How Much Mail Do They Send?

Table 2.1 summarizes the total message traffic of the organizations surveyed. Of significance are:

- The tremendous volume, almost 150 million pieces per day in the United States alone;

- The low proportion currently carried by electronic means (telex and facsimile)—less than 4% in the Federal Republic of Germany, which had the highest percentage;

---

*These establishments employ the majority of white collar and professional workers in the United States and Western Europe. In Europe they account for 50% to 60% of all mail carried by the PTTs, and in the United States for 43% of the business and government mail carried by the U.S. Postal Service (USPS).

Table 2.1 Total Mail Volume Per Day for Four Countries (millions of items)

	France	Federal Republic of Germany	U.K.	U.S.
Total	23.6	24.7	24.0	146.8
Facsimile	0.03	0.03	0.04	NA
Telex	0.32	0.91	0.48	1.0*
Intra-organizational	3.1	1.76	2.28	41.1

NA: Not available
*Western Union estimate

Source: Mackintosh International and Communication Studies and Planning Ltd., 1979.

- The high proportion of intraorganizational mail (the kind most easily converted to electronic mail)—28% in the United States, and 10% in Europe.

The majority of organizations in our sample had a moderate to low volume of mail. In France, where patterns of use were typical of European trends, 78% of firms sent between 50 to 200 pieces daily. (See Figure 2.1.) Volume in the United States was even lower: 73% of firms sent less than 50 pieces.

However, the very small number of firms which send more than 200 pieces per day, less than 6% of the whole sample, *account for more than all of the others put together—well over 60%.*

The pattern of intraorganizational mail is similar. As one would expect, most firms have only a single branch, or handle intraorganizational communications by telephone. Thus, a majority send no intraorganizational mail at all. Of the remainder, most send a few items, while a small minority of organizations send the bulk of it: *2% of organizations in the United States send 71% of all intraorganizational mail.* (Figure 2.2 illustrates this distribution.)

What Means Do They Use?

The organizations in our survey relied on traditional postal services for the vast majority of their mail needs. There was considerable national variation, however, ranging from 74% of items being sent by post in France and the United Kingdom, to 96% in the Federal Republic of Germany, where private courier services are banned by law. Not surprisingly, first class mail is the most popular of these services.

Figure 2.1 Percentage of Organizations Sending Different Volumes of Mail (France)

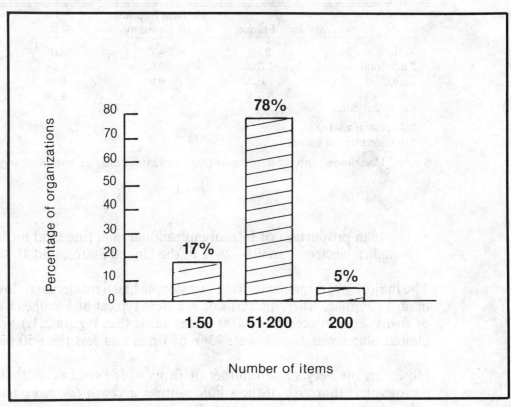

Source: Mackintosh International and Communication Studies and Planning Ltd., 1978.

Significantly (except in Germany), non-postal mail services—messengers, commercial delivery services and internal van/car delivery—make up considerable proportion of mail volume, as much as 19% in the U.K. (See Table 2.2.) The pattern of delivery for intraorganizational mail differs markedly from that for interorganizational mail, with alternatives to post being used more frequently. Table 2.3 presents this comparison for the United States.

What Do They Send?

Here we are interested in the rather narrowly drawn question of the physical characteristics of mail. The most obvious one is whether an item must be physically transmitted, which is the case for books, periodicals, merchandise

Figure 2.2 Intraorganizational Mail (U.S.)

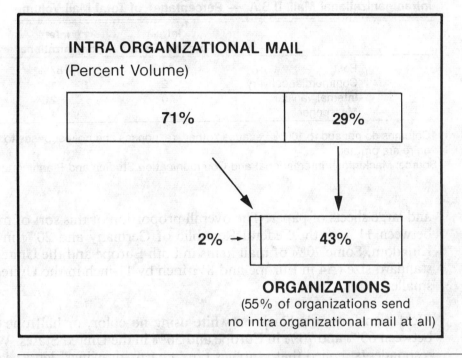

Source: Mackintosh International and Communication Studies and Planning Ltd., 1978.

Table 2.2 Methods of Delivery — Percentage* of Total Mail Volume

	France	Federal Republic of Germany	U.K.	U.S.
Post	74%	96%	74%	84%
(First class only)	(48)	(92)†	(38)	(72)
Commercial delivery	1	—	1	1
Internal van/car	5	1	11	2
Messenger	2	1	7	3

*Columns do not add to 100% because "other" responses and no-responses to the questionnaire are omitted.

†Federal Republic of Germany offers no second class service.

Source: Mackintosh International and Communication Studies and Planning Ltd., 1978.

Table 2.3 Methods of Delivery — Interorganizational Versus Intraorganizational Mail, U.S.A. — Percentage* of Total Mail Volume

	Intra-organizational	Inter-organizational
Post	61%	87%
Commercial delivery	2	1
Internal van/car	10	2
Messenger	15	1

*Columns do not add to 100% because "other" responses and no-responses to the questionnaire are omitted.

Source: Mackintosh International and Communication Studies and Planning Ltd., 1978.

and large sheets of paper. The overall proportion of this sort of mail is small: between 11% in the Federal Republic of Germany and 20% in the United Kingdom. Some 70% of mail items in both Europe and the United States are standard size (A4 in Europe and 8½-inch by 11-inch in the United States) or smaller.

Most items are only black on white using no color, or halftone (i.e., grey): between 60% and 70% in Europe and 56% in the United States. When asked, respondents replied that graphics (i.e., charts, drawings, letterheads, printed overlays) are unnecessary for 80% of items sampled in the United States, and for more than 70% in Europe. Of those items which needed graphics, letterhead or overlay were required by about a third and full graphics by the rest. High-quality printing on the other hand—of the quality of a good electric typewriter or better—was required by a high proportion of all items: between 45% and 60%.

IMPLICATIONS FOR ELECTRONIC MAIL

From the previous discussion we can draw a number of conclusions about electronic mail system design.

The physical characteristics of mail items imply that even the simplest electronic mail devices (those which can handle only text in black and white) are suitable for a large proportion of mail, *if* they can provide reasonably high print quality. However, additional items can be handled with the addition of graphics capability.

The information on volume ("How much do they send?") and method of delivery ("What means do they use?") requires more subtle analysis. The volume survey reveals two sorts of users: those with small to medium volumes (the vast majority of users), and those with very large volumes. The justification for electronic mail in each of the two sorts of user organizations may be quite different.

For the low volume user, conversion to electronic mail will be relatively easy—a single terminal (probably telex or facsimile) and a part-time operator will do. Nevertheless, the expenditure on standard postal services will be so low that the fixed cost of even a small installation cannot be justified on postal costs alone. Instead, either careful accounting of the cost of special services—messengers, commercial delivery services or express mail—must be made, or justification must be based on increased convenience and productivity.

For high volume users, cost justification may be possible strictly on the basis of routine mail usage—particularly in the case of intraorganizational mail where conversion is relatively easy. However, the installations for high volume users will tend to be more complex, and require higher investment.

DETERMINING DESIRABLE FEATURES FOR ELECTRONIC MAIL SYSTEMS

The previous discussion has illuminated a number of constraints on electronic mail arising from the types and number of items transmitted. Many of the other necessary features of electronic mail derive not from the nature of the items but from user needs: matters of convenience, speed and security. Electronic mail systems must accommodate these needs, which are fundamentally social and organizational, just as much as the physical characteristics of mail items. Since user perceptions play the critical role in defining the needs, we will examine them first. Based on these and other considerations we set forth a number of features electronic mail system can usefully include. We based this discussion on the results of the interview survey which formed part of our study program.

User Perceptions Regarding Existing Delivery Systems

Satisfaction with Current Mail Services

User satisfaction with current mail services varies in different countries; a function, presumably, of the quality of the national postal service, among other factors. Most users in the United States expressed dissatisfaction with the quality of first-class service on the basis of its slow speed and unreliability. In Germany, about half of the users interviewed expressed general satisfaction while the other half criticized the service for being too slow. Service in France and the U.K. was generally well regarded although there were specific, minor complaints. In general, most users were not dissatisfied with the cost of the post. A small minority in the United Kingdom was the only significant exception.

Satisfaction with TWX and Telex

Telex presented a more complex picture. In the United States, most users were generally satisfied with telex/TWX service, although a minority of customers complained about equipment unreliability. There was, however, little criticism of the service concept. In Europe, the impression was less positive. The most common complaint was of the difficulty in making international calls: long delays in getting a line and misrouting were alleged to be regular, if not frequent, occurrences. Other, less common criticisms concerned telex's limited character set, poor printing quality and the noise of terminals. Nonusers of telex systems frequently complained that the service was too expensive for their business.

Satisfaction with Facsimile Services

Facsimile showed a similar pattern of response on different sides of the Atlantic, although the use of facsimile equipment is much more widespread in the United States than in Europe. Most U.S. facsimile users expressed general satisfaction with the system, although poor paper handling and copy quality were cited as problems by some. In Europe, poor quality of reproduction was widely reported, as were limitations owing to the lack of compatibility standards between different manufacturers and the small number of installed terminals (which restricted intercompany use).

Examining the Data: What Users Want

The pattern which emerges from these interviews is that there is wide variation among different users in their attitudes toward mail service. A large number of users are unwilling to pay the premium that is necessary for conventional alternatives that provide better services. For example, first-class mail was most often criticized for its slowness in the United States, yet its usage there is as high as, or higher than, in most other countries examined. Excessive cost was frequently cited as a reason for not using telex. Other users, however, depended heavily on telex and premium courier services, and paid heavily for them.

Thus, speed can command a premium for some users and for some items, but not for others; each user strikes his own balance between the two factors, cost and speed. Current electronic alternatives to conventional post are relegated to specialized uses largely because they fall to only one side of this balance. However, as the next chapter will discuss, the cost of offering current levels of service in electronic mail is dropping rapidly and will shift the balance in favor of electronic methods for many more users. Still, each user will have to judge this individually.

The most frequent complaints about existing electronic alternatives involved convenience and utility—poor paper handling and high rates of call rejection were among the problems cited. From these and other complaints, we have derived the following list of features necessary for broad acceptance of electronic mail. (See Figure 2.3.) Although many of these features are currently unavailable, all will be technically feasible at reasonable cost by the mid-1980s.

Figure 2.3 Features of Electronic Mail Systems Necessary for Broad Acceptance

- Store-and-forward capability
- Unattended reception
- Simultaneous message preparation/transmission
- Wide compatibility
- Security
- Privacy

Store-and-Forward Capability

Systems must allow *store-and-forward capability*. High call rejection rate was the most frequent complaint by European telex users. One reason for this is that a telex connection must be completed before a message may be sent, just as a telephone must be answered before one may speak. But what makes sense for a telephone, which is a two-way medium, makes no sense at all for telex or electronic mail. If the called terminal is busy, the system should be able to store the message somewhere until the terminal is free, at which point the system automatically forwards the message. Otherwise, operators must redial calls each time a called terminal is busy. Moreover, since cost rather than speed is often the primary consideration, a system should allow messages to be sent during off-peak periods at reduced cost. Since the best time for this is late at night, in the absence of store-and-forward any transmission savings would be offset by the wage-premiums you would have to pay a night operator.

Of course, high speed delivery can be provided at premium rates, but even here a short delay is usually acceptable (say, 15 minutes). To some extent, even more important than the absolute speed of delivery is that the delivery time be guaranteed; one of the most common complaints against conventional post is its unreliability rather than its slowness.

Unattended Reception and Simultaneous Message Preparation/Transmission

Similarly, the system must allow unattended reception, and simultaneous message preparation/transmission. As a one-way medium, electronic mail should not require an operator to be present for the message to be received (yet most facsimile systems now require this). This is especially critical for international users, where time zone differences reduce the likelihood of sender and receiver being present at the same time. Simultaneous message preparation and transmission eliminates messages being rejected by the system due to terminals being engaged in preparation of outgoing text. Telex systems do not provide this facility, and this, along with the lack of store-and-forward capability, accounts for the majority of rejected calls.

The Need for System Compatibility

A system must be widely compatible among different users. As we have seen, this is already perceived as a significant problem among many facsimile users. Clearly, too, the value of any mail system is limited if a high proportion of the people to whom we want to send messages are inaccessible. There is a similar need for directories of electronic mail users since, for use to become widespread, users who are not known to each other must be able to communicate. This is another reason why electronic mail systems will first develop to serve intraorganizational communications.

Making the System Secure

In addition to these specific features derived from user interviews, a general consideration for any mail system is that it be secure. Confirmation of delivery is an essential feature for many applications, as is the knowledge that a message is delivered intact, and that it cannot be easily forged or altered.

These considerations are often built-in features of conventional mail systems. Security is provided by the physical characteristics of the item—the fact that conventional mail items, e.g., letters or checks, are difficult to alter or forge, and that loss of some part of a message requires physical destruction. In electronic mail, messages are electronic impulses which are easy to manipulate, and may disappear without a trace. Therefore, special consideration of these problems is appropriate here.

Technical safeguards do exist. Terminals and networks can be provided with error detection and correction logic so that transmission is error free. Networks can be designed so that very important messages are "echoed" back to the sender, allowing him to check for correct delivery. Notification of delivery can also be provided at lower cost through the incorporation of simple logic. This feature is already built-in in the telex service, through transmission of the answer back code at the end of the message.

Authorization is an additional concern since the conventions adopted in physical transmission—based on the presence of an original signature—do not transfer easily to electronic mail. A simple solution is for the transmission network to provide a location code for the originating terminal on the message. For many purposes this would be adequate; for example, for intra-organizational use, knowledge that an internal memo originated from a terminal in headquarters would suffice. For more sensitive applications, security analogous to that of a signature could be provided by personal identifiers which could be included in a message only if the sender knew a private password.

The Importance of Privacy

A final concern is privacy. Electronic messages can be monitored, although encryption (or coding) devices are well developed and could be adopted at reasonable cost. However this presents difficulty for some international traffic, where encryption is illegal. Most electronic messages will not arrive in envelopes, but will be printed on terminals. For this reason, passwords and keywords are likely to become standard techniques for insuring that the person who receives a message is in fact authorized to see it.

SUMMARY

This analysis of mail usage and user perceptions has provided a basis for understanding user needs. Later discussions will amplify this analysis, and draw it more explicitly into the electronic mail context. But a number of points are already clear:

- The opportunity for a sizable volume of mail items to be diverted to electronic transmission exists.

- The simplest sort of system, text-only electronic mail, is adequate for a broad range of uses, although graphics capability would extend usefulness.

- High costs and the lack of features such as store-and-forward currently block wider adoption of electronic mail use.

3

The Technology of Electronic Mail

In the previous chapter we discussed user needs and system features without reference to costs, and with only limited reference to technology. The function of this chapter is to fill in these gaps concerning electronic mail hardware. The economics of use are discussed in subsequent chapters.

The emphasis throughout will be on explanation, not just description. For hardware alone is not the key to understanding electronic mail, or to appreciating its impact, which will be felt increasingly in the next decade. Indeed, most of the elements of an integrated electronic mail system have been technically possible for at least 10 years. Instead, it is the combination of technology and price which, for the first time, makes the cost of using these systems competitive as compared to their conventional alternatives.

THE MICROELECTRONICS REVOLUTION

The driving force behind this movement toward competitiveness for electronic mail has been the dramatic drop in price of some of its more sophisticated elements. There are the circuits that allow text manipulation in word processors, and allow facsimile machines to work more efficiently and their output to be stored and switched. Many of these circuits were developed for computer applications; in fact, a modern word processor has much in common with a small general purpose computer, though the word processor has been programmed for a specific use.

Large-scale Integration

The technique that allows these circuits to be made economically is called large-scale integration (LSI). In this process, tens of thousands of separate electronic components and connecting pathways are created by microscopically etching alternating layers of silicon and insulating materials. (Silicon is the basic material of transistors.) A similar technique made possible the portable electronic calculator and the digital quartz watch, along with the dramatic drop in price both have experienced. The same sort of trend is now developing for LSI techniques, so that a whole central processor, the heart of a computer, can easily be placed on a single "chip" (the colloquial name for these circuits).

To describe this development as revolutionary is not an overstatement. The effect of LSI has already been seen in computers, where the processing power that even 10 years ago would have cost as much as $100,000 may now be purchased for a few thousand dollars. However, development has not been limited to standard computer applications. A complete processing unit, called a microprocessor, now costs less than $10 to buy in volume. By 1985, the price will have fallen to less than $2. (See Figure 3.1.) Even though other essential components, such as a power supply, memory and peripherals are necessary for these processors to be useful, it will be possible, as a result, to include enormous processing power in a wide range of consumer goods. Of most interest to us, however, is that the use of microprocessors in office products, which has already been economic on a moderate scale, will become increasingly more attractive.

In addition to processors, LSI will have an important impact on electronic mail by decreasing the cost of electronic memory. Here the advances may seem even more dramatic than in the case of processors. The cost of standard random access memory (RAM) chips is declining by 30% to 40% a year. This will have important implications both for terminals and for network memory requirements such as store-and-forward capability.

PRINTING, IMAGING, DISPLAY AND OTHER TECHNIQUES

As dramatic as these changes in the cost and performance of microelectronic circuits are, they do not affect every component of an electronic mail system, and therefore do not completely determine trends in the total price of such systems. Obviously, the electronic impulses with which microcircuits work are not visible to the eye — they require display or printing. Similarly, the impulses don't just materialize, they must be entered — in the case of facsimile, through "imaging," the creation of an electronic representation of a picture, or in the case of text, through the use of a keyboard. Also, we may wish to preserve the information for an extended period of time, perhaps to file it away. If we save it in electronic form, we require peripheral memory. Many of these other elements of an electronic mail system use integrated circuits in only part of their design — the other components might be mechanical, or involve other forms of electronics.

Figure 3.1 Volume Price Trend Projections for Microprocessor Chips

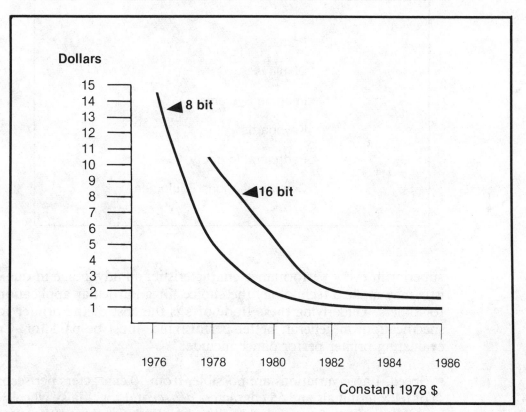

Source: Mackintosh International and Communication Studies and Planning Ltd., 1978.

In this section we will discuss the functional elements of an electronic mail system, and examine the technological basis of each (See Figure 3.2.). We will look at printing, imaging, display and memory techniques that do not depend exclusively on integrated circuit technologies, and will also touch on the communications interface and the line unit, which connects the terminal to the telecommunications line.

Printing

There are literally dozens of printing techniques that can be applied to electronic mail. They exist simultaneously because there is no one type which is

Figure 3.2 Functional Elements of Electronic Mail Systems

```
        *   Printers

        *   Displays

        *   Imaging Systems

        *   Keyboards

        *   Peripheral Memory

        *   Communications Equipment
```

superior in every performance characteristic: an advantage in one characteristic may make a technology the choice for a particular application, but not for others. Underlying these trade-offs is the cost of the printer for a given specification: in general, better performance must be paid for. Criteria for evaluating printer performance include:

- Speed. Large variations are possible, from 10 characters per second typical of telex terminals and 55 characters per second for "daisy wheel" machines — both of which are suitable for relatively low priced units — to very expensive machines printing over 21,000 *lines* per minute. Obviously, the choice of printer speed depends on the expected volume of use.

- Print quality. Here the variation ranges from legible to excellent — to as good, say, as the best electric office typewriter.

- Graphics capability. The simplest printers are based on typewriter-like mechanisms, and are limited to text-only. Graphics capability necessitates extra sophistication.

- Consumption of supplies. A number of printers require specially treated paper or other special supplies. In general, these printers cost less than plain-paper printers of similar performance. However, coated paper itself will usually cost more than plain bond, may deteriorate over time, and may be deemed unattractive, so that where volumes are high or other considerations are important, plain-paper terminals may offer better value.

Impact vs. Non-impact Printers

Printer technologies are of several different types. A fundamental distinction is between impact and non-impact printers. Impact printers, like typewriters, generally strike an inked ribbon to leave an impression on paper. The type might be on a "golf ball," like the head on an IBM Selectric typewriter, or on a "daisy wheel" which has characters on the ends of the radial spokes of a wheel. Alternatively, the typeset may not be fixed, but made up of adjustable dots which, like the lights of a scoreboard making up letters and numbers, define characters by selective printing of the different points (so-called matrix printers).

Non-impact printers use a number of techniques to produce images on paper. Some, called electrostatic printers, use a process very much like photocopying. As with copiers, some machines use plain paper (there are indirect electrostatic printers) and others use coated paper (direct electrostatic). Another kind of printer, the ink-jet printer, actually sprays ink onto the paper. The ink is electrically charged, so that the shape of the character can be controlled electronically by deflecting the path of the ink stream as it passes through a variable magnetic field.

The slower impact and ink-jet mechanisms print one character at a time. Thus, printers depending on these technologies can be speeded up by building into them more than one mechanism for printing, so that the processes occur in parallel. For example, some impact printers have a separate print hammer for every character position on the line. Table 3.1 summarizes the main characteristics of various forms of printers.

In general, impact printers (e.g., daisy wheel, matrix and parallel impact printers) currently provide the best techniques for low-to-medium speed high quality applications. However, ink-jet is already competitive in this range and can be expected to improve in both cost and performance. Non-impact electrostatic printers offer the best performance in the very high speed range, and some are cost-competitive with the fastest impact techniques. All non-impact techniques share a drawback of being unable to produce multiple carbon-copies, while direct electrostatic techniques require coated paper. Thus, impact and non-impact techniques are likely to coexist for the foreseeable future, but with ink-jet and electrostatic mechanisms taking a larger and larger market share.

It is clear that much of the development in printer technology will be in the area of non-impact techniques. This is because the role of electronic circuitry

Table 3.1 Characteristics of Competing Printer Technologies

Type printer	Maximum speed	Print quality	Graphics capability	Cost of supplies	Fixed cost
IMPACT PRINTERS					
Daisy wheel	55 cps*	High	No	Medium	Low
Matrix	400 cps*	Medium to High	Some	Low	Low
Parallel impact	3000 lpm†	Medium	No	Low	Medium to High
NON-IMPACT PRINTERS					
Ink-jet (single)	300 cps*	High	Yes	Low	Low to Medium
Direct electrostatic (coated paper)	21,000 lpm†	High	Yes	Medium to High	Medium to High
Indirect electrostatic (plain paper)	21,000 lpm†	High	Yes	Low	High

*cps = characters per second

† lpm = lines per minute

is more important in non-impact printers, which can thus take advantage of the continuing developments and cost reductions in electronic component technology and production.

Display Techniques

A display allows text to be viewed without printing. Its most important use is for editing, when it shows the operator what has been entered and if changes have been made. A secondary, but also important use, is as a substitute for printing complete messages. In some circumstances printing is necessary, as for example when a document must be taken away from the office, but for most uses a display is all that is necessary. However, it will be some years before office workers lose the "paper" habits they have acquired.

Displays exist for single lines, multiple lines, whole pages of text and for text and graphics. For single lines of text a matrix display composed of light emitting diodes is most common. (This is the same technology used in many calculators and early digital watches.) The letters are formed by turning on the appropriate dots (diodes). The technology currently used for most digital watches (liquid crystal display) can also be used very effectively.

Cathode Ray Tube (CRT)

For all applications requiring more than a few words there is no substitute for the cathode ray tube (CRT), which is the picture device used in television receivers. The resolution and flicker reduction requirements of electronic mail may, for some applications, exceed those needed for a television picture and lead to a requirement for a better CRT than found in television sets.

A state-of-the-art CRT is capable of resolving 4000 lines across the screen (TV tubes scan at 525 or 625), but a tube of this quality is generally too costly for an electronic mail terminal. Thus CRTs of various quality levels are used, depending on the price of the terminal. The advantages of a better display are that the more lines scanned, the more legible the characters, and the smaller they may be.* This is important because poor resolution is fatiguing for the operator, and because displays showing more characters at a time may be more convenient.

Although there will be further improvements to the CRT, the technology has been in use too long to expect any more major advances. There is research work being done on other display technologies but major breakthroughs are not expected in the near future. It is unlikely that the cathode ray tube will have any serious competitor until the late 1980s, if then.

Imaging Techniques

Just as printing and electronic display are the two ways in which the contents of electronic mail are made visible, imaging is one of two general ways in which the contents are entered (the other is the keyboard). Imaging is, simply, the creation of an electronic representation of the visual elements of a document.

In facsimile terminals a page is "scanned," i.e., it is broken up into a number of horizontal lines, spaced at regular intervals, in much the same way as a single frame of a TV picture. Choosing the technology for horizontal and vertical scanning represents a compromise between speed, resolution, cost and reliability.

The scanning function may be accomplished in one of two ways. A spot of

---

*A good rule-of-thumb for judging the quality of a display is that each character requires about 9 lines vertically and 7 "dots" horizontally. Adding in 4 lines and 3 dots for inter-line and inter-character spaces, means that each line of type to be displayed requires 13 scanning lines, and each character position requires a horizontal resolution of 10 dots.

light can traverse the page and a "wideview" detector can be used to detect the fraction of light reflected from the page. Or, the page can be illuminated generally and a line projected onto a scanning detector, such as a charge-couple device (CCD) or a photodiode array. The first method of scanning is the one generally adopted in current analog units. The second sort of scanning technique is suited to digital representation.

Charge-coupled devices and photodiodes are capable of being produced through techniques analogous to large-scale integration, and thus will benefit from dramatic cost reductions in the near future. CCD chips, for example, which cost about $1000 in 1978, should drop to the $50 to $100 range by the early 1980s. Additionally, if a medium/high volume market develops, prices should drop even lower.

Keyboards and Voice Entry of Text

Keyboards are currently the most common method for entering information into a system and this is likely to remain so. The most technologically advanced keyboards need little more improvement, except for the ergonomics.* However the market will see further advances in reliability and cost reduction since most of the keyboards presently in use do not include all the recent advances and can be improved.

Keyboard ergonomics can be greatly improved, especially for keyboards used by untrained operators. In the course of the last 20 years there have been numerous attempts to build keyboards that can be operated without extensive training but none have acquired wide acceptance.

Voice operated input has been achieved for small vocabularies and research is continuing. Most of the systems built up to now have proved to be too costly for office use, and have insufficient vocabularies. It is possible that the continued advances in software and fall in the price of electronics may make a "dictation-typewriter" practical late in the next decade.

OTHER TECHNOLOGICAL COMPONENTS OF ELECTRONIC MAIL TERMINALS

The printing, imaging and display techniques already described make up many of the important elements of an electronic mail terminal. Most other

---

*Ergonomics, or human factors engineering, is the science of designing machines, operations and work environments that best meet the needs of the workers involved with them.

components, like cabinets and paper-handling systems, employ familiar technologies which are unlikely to improve except for economies of production. Two exceptions should be mentioned here: peripheral memory and communications interfaces.

Peripheral Memory

Memory is used for three related but distinct functions in electronic mail. The first is to store the programs that instruct the terminal in its operation; the second is to hold the text or image during the period it is being worked on (entered and edited); and the third is to act as a file or archive and as a "bulk" memory. It is this last function which is called peripheral memory, although there tends to be overlap between the equipment used for these functions in a practical installation.*

For bulk memory it is convenient to use a technology that allows the memory medium (e.g., a magnetic disc) to be removed for physical storage when it is full. It is also very important that bulk memory *not* depend upon the terminal power supply, otherwise the stored text will be lost if the terminal is turned off or if the power supply fails.

Some bulk-memory devices are fully electronic; more commonly they are electromechanical, and work on the same principles as do tape recorders, or any other magnetic recording device. In fact, one of the cheapest devices for this purpose is a slightly modified audiocassette drive. This is quite adequate for long term storage where editing is completed, and input/output (I/O) speed is unimportant.

More sophisticated devices are necessary when editing is involved, or input/output speed is important. One of the most common of these devices is the floppy disc; so named because the magnetic coating is placed on a flexible plastic disc. Small rigid discs are also available, and becoming increasingly popular. In use, a floppy disc is spun at about 300 rpm. Information is recorded on the surface of the disc in separate, concentric rings, called tracks, by a read/write head which moves in and out on a radial axis. Thus, each track can be read or re-recorded separately, with delay being a function of the time it takes to move the head to the proper track, plus the time it takes for the disc to come around to the beginning (on average, 1/600 of a minute). Rigid discs work very much the same way, but generally spin faster and have

---

*For programs it is usual to use integrated circuits, but some manufacturers put less frequently used programs in the "bulk store." In working memory, integrated circuits are also used but of a different type.

higher capacity. The capacity of any disc is limited by the density at which information can be written on the track, and the number of tracks that can be placed on a single disc. Improvements are likely in both of these areas, which will help reduce the cost per character stored. This, coupled with better production methods and economies of large-scale production, will reduce the cost by an order of magnitude in 1985, compared to prices prevailing in 1978.

Communications Equipment

An important part of any electronic mail terminal is the communications equipment that connects it to the transmission network. This equipment transforms the internal representation of the information to a form that is capable of being transmitted. This equipment consists of a communications interface which presents the bits and control signals in a suitable form, and a modem which converts the signals to a form an analog communications line can accept. On some networks (i.e., digital data networks) the modem is unnecessary, but over the normal telephone line both sorts of manipulation are necessary. If, for example, a character is represented by eight bits of information, the eight bits must be converted to a series of pulses in time. This is done by the communications interface.

If the signal is going to be sent over the telephone network the pulses must be converted to tones; a low frequency tone for a 0 and a high frequency tone for a 1. This is done by the modem. At the other end of the line, this process must be reversed. Various types of communications equipment differ by the speeds at which they operate, the "protocols" they use for conversion and the degree to which they use "intelligence" to maintain contact.

An intelligent modem can tell when contact has been made, and can select automatically from among several different conversion conventions to one that is compatible with the modem at the other end.

Advanced modems have built-in error detection and correction circuitry that allows data transmission to occur at the highest rate at which the lines will allow. A bad connection will cause a high rate of errors, and the system will slow down; a good connection will allow it to speed up.

Since many of these functions can be incorporated into single microelectronic circuits, their cost will drop throughout the foreseeable future.

As we have seen, the cost of many of the individual units of electronic mail is declining, at the same time that performance is improving. This would suggest that terminal and transmission systems will do a better job for the same cost, or even for less cost, and this is indeed what we expect. We will discuss terminals and transmission systems separately in making projections for a variety of different kinds of electronic mail.

COST AND PERFORMANCE PROJECTIONS FOR TERMINALS

Much of the dramatic drop in component prices will be used to improve the performance of electronic mail terminals rather than to lower their price. Several factors account for this. Marketing costs, particularly in the early 1980s when the market is relatively undeveloped, will be high. Performance of current electronic mail terminals leaves a great deal of room for improvement: amortized over the life of a machine, performance improvement will more than justify an increased cost over a basic machine sold at a low price. Yet, by the end of the 1980s, competitive pressures will have resulted in a substantial improvement in cost compared to current prices.

Facsimile Systems

The area in which facsimile machines may be improved include: better image quality, easier document feeding, higher reliability, more security safeguards and lower transmission times.

Three general classes of machines currently on the market can be identified, although particularly in North America the groups are not as distinct as would appear here, and other options exist:

- Group 1: Analog machines which take about six minutes per page, and can produce both black and white and shades of grey (i.e., grey-scale).

- Group 2: Also analog machines with transmission time less than three minutes per page, and permitting grey-scale.

- Group 3: Digital machines with average transmission time of less than one minute per page, but capable of only black on white reproduction (no grey).

Group 1 and Group 2 Machines

The technology employed by Group 1 machines is already mature, and little improvement in performance and price can be expected. New products in

Group 2 will typically give better image quality (some of the newest Group 2 machines use ink-jet printing technology to permit the use of plain paper), easier document feeding, and more security safeguards, as well as being more reliable. But this will arise mainly from products incorporating the better features of some current machines rather than technological advance.

Group 3 Machines

It is within Group 3 that the most innovation will occur. However, even here the trend will be evolutionary, using technology that is already in use for facsimile or is currently employed for copiers. Print quality, using electrostatic or ink-jet technologies, will improve with higher contrast and cleaner appearance. Transmission times will be reduced, partly because of better modem design, and the likelihood that the line will work at higher speeds, and partly by improved intelligence in the terminal. This will allow "white line skipping," where machines skip the bit-by-bit transmission of white lines or gaps, and send instead a short code to mark the location and size of the area. In addition, Group 3 machines will permit the inclusion of electronic memory, allowing store-and-forward from the terminal.

Group 4 and Group 5 Machines

It is quite likely that two new groups of facsimile machines will appear in the next decade. One of these, which may be called Group 4, will be intended to work with combined text and graphic systems. (The Teletex Standard, discussed in Chapter 5, will provide for machines that can handle both messages and facsimile transmission.) The other new group, perhaps called Group 5, will be digital machines intended to operate over leased data lines. The rate of data transmission of these machines will be five to 10 times faster than for Group 3 machines, and for the same quality. It is also likely that they will allow the user to specify higher resolution or grey-scale for some documents (at the cost of longer transmission time). An attractive additional feature of Group 5 machines is that their high speed will make them suitable to double as standard office copiers at relatively low extra cost, although if standard copying loads are heavy, use as a terminal may not be desirable.

Specific projections for the average rental of Groups 1 to 3 in the United States are shown in Figure 3.3. As can be seen, competition will force Group 2 rental prices down by the early 1980s, although the decline will be moderated by the performance improvements already discussed. By the mid 1980s, the wide availability of Group 3 machines will have eroded the market for feature-rich Group 2 machines, although some demand will be preserved by customers who need grey-scale capability, or have only moderate traffic.

Toward the end of the 1980s, the Group 2 market will be heavily eroded by the introduction of very low cost Group 3 machines, with and without store-and-forward capability.

Figure 3.3 Average Monthly Rental of Facsimile Terminals on Public Switched Telephone Network (PSTN) Lines (U.S.), 1980-1987

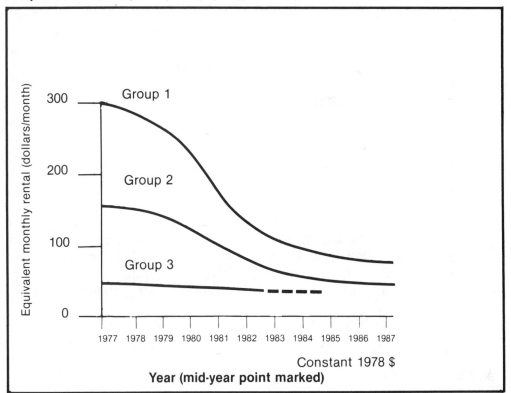

Source: Mackintosh International and Communications Studies and Planning Ltd., 1978.

Text Systems

The key to understanding the further development of text systems is the fact that electronic mail capacity can be a low cost add-on to investment in word processing, which is already occurring rapidly. Many businesses are able to justify the purchase of these systems on the basis of productivity improvements to typing alone. With text systems, editing and turn-around time are reduced, form letters can be personalized and final copy can be perfect. Most of the expensive elements of a text-only electronic mail system are necessary for a word processing system anyway: the printing mechanism, keyboard, much of the software and almost all of the electronics. What is necessary to convert these systems to electronic mail terminals is the communications equipment, a small amount of additional software for the processor, and a transmission line, which is likely to be the existing telephone line for external communication, or an internal coaxial cable for messages within a single building.

We can distinguish two kinds of word processing systems currently being marketed:

- Stand-alone: these are functionally most like standard office typewriters, with the addition of electronic editing facilities.

- Clustered systems: those which have a number of terminals with shared facilities. For example, what are essentially stand-alone systems may be connected by an internal communications system, allowing them to share printers or bulk memory. In other systems, all of the keyboards might share the same, powerful processor* as well as peripherals.

Some general trends are likely for all types of word processing systems. Within the processor, larger working memories will be fitted. Outside the processor, printing technology will be the area of greatest improvement — in particular the further development and adoption of non-impact systems such as ink-jet or electrographic. Keyboards will undergo a steady improvement, with the reduction of mechanical switching giving higher reliability.

There will be other developments specific to clustered or stand-alone word processing systems, and we will look at each in turn.

Stand-alone Systems

It is almost certain that the drop in price of large-scale integrated circuits and bulk memory will allow manufacturers to produce very low cost stand-alone processors. A likely marketing strategy would be to sell a basic electronic typewriter with separate add-on modules for upgrading to more complex functions. The basic configuration will likely cost little more than a standard office typewriter, so that virtually every office will be able to justify its purchase on the basis of improved typing efficiency. These machines will not,

---

*The microelectronics revolution described earlier has given cost advantage to smaller, single-chip processors. The trend, therefore, is toward clustered systems which share peripherals, but distribute processing among a number of separate microprocessors.

however, be capable of communication without add-on modules which will add to the basic cost.

By the early to mid-1980s, competition will force prices down to a quasi-stable low point, when manufacturing costs will be strongly influenced by the cost of the mechanical parts and the marketing will have been streamlined. This will apply to both communicating and non-communicating models. (See Figure 3.4.)

One development that will assist low cost communication will be the *offline text/data communicator*. This is a separate unit that will allow an operator to remove the floppy disc, cassette or other peripheral memory from his word processor, insert it into the offline communicator and dial or key in the destination. The communicator has enough intelligence to handle the communication and the message will be sent when a device at the other end of the line establishes contact and signals that it is ready. For receiving, the operator

Figure 3.4 Average Monthly Rental of a Stand-Alone Word Processor with a CRT Display (U.S.), 1978-87

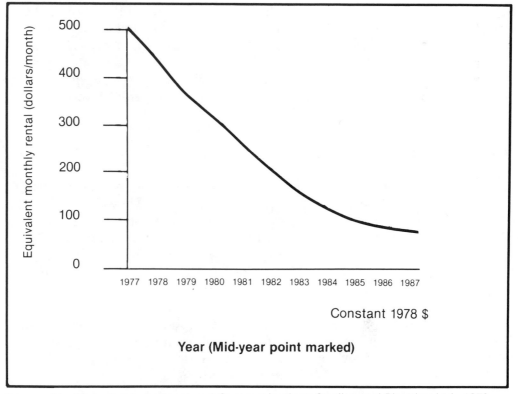

Source: Mackintosh International and Communications Studies and Planning Ltd., 1978.

would insert a blank floppy disc or cassette. Offline communicators will thus offer a cheap, if somewhat inconvenient, means of communication for a user with several basic word processors and low electronic mail traffic.

Clustered Systems

During the late 1980s, integrated in-house communication systems will become common. By linking all of the electronic equipment in an office, efficient utilization of peripherals will be maximized and a large number of office tasks will be automated. Filing, for example, will be economically handled by a bulk-memory central store eliminating paper handling, and allowing for automatic search and retrieval. Printing will become a separate function because the word processor operator will no longer need paper in many instances.

There will be a blurring of the distinction between "word" processing and "data" processing. More and more business computing functions will be incorporated into these systems, so that more businesses may find word processing cost-justified if they require data processing anyway.

In the early 1980s, the overall performance of this class of word processor will rise, accompanied by further increases in intelligence. The related price trend will be, for a given performance standard, an initial slow fall gaining in momentum to the mid-1980s and thereafter slowing. Where business computing features are added, prices will tend to rise, although for those machines too, prices will drop in the late 1980s. (Figure 3.5 shows this projection.)

Hybrid Terminals

The most dramatic innovation that we expect in the early 1980s will be the introduction of *text-and-graphics* terminals. These combine the capabilities of both communicating word processors and digital facsimile machines. Text-and-graphics terminals will be capable of receiving messages from either of these two types of devices, and will be able to send messages in text mode to standard communicating word processors and in facsimile mode to, for example, Group 3 facsimile machines.

Input would be via a scanner, or a keyboard, and special graphic functions — such as insertion of a letterhead — could be preprogrammed to work at the push of a button. All printing would take place on a "scanning" printer. Graphics would be printed directly as in facsimile, and text indirectly via a character generator.

Figure 3.5 Average Monthly Rental (Per Work Station) of a Clustered Word Processor (U.S.), 1978-87

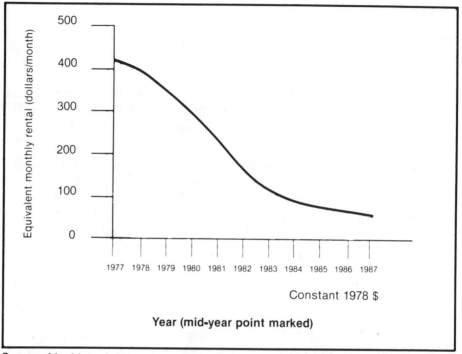

Source: Mackintosh International and Communications Studies and Planning Ltd., 1978.

Overall costs for a hybrid terminal will be lower than the costs of a communicating word processor plus Group 3 facsimile because the printer and some electronics could be shared between them. Optical character readers could be added, which would allow the automatic conversion to text representation for scanned, original documents containing printed text. Advanced models would allow text and graphics to be mixed on a page, using graphics mode, for example, to transmit a company logo, and switching to the more economical text transmission for the body of the document.

Initial Problems

Major problems in the early development of text-and-graphics terminals will be a lack of compatibility standards between products of different manufacturers, and the design of software and other features to make operation convenient. Initially, any fall in manufacturing costs is likely to be offset by the high costs of marketing. Eventually however, when competition has built up, lower manufacturing costs will lead to improved performance and, for a few products, lower sales or rental prices.

It is likely that by the late 1980s, the hybrid terminal will supersede the communicating word processor and digital facsimile machine for general purpose use.

RELATED DEVELOPMENTS — VIDEOTEXT

A parallel development during the 1980s involves the potential expansion of videotext (viewdata) systems from AT&T in the U.S., British Telecom in the U.K. and other telephone companies in other countries.

Videotext is generally conceived as a data base access method: users dial up a central computer that sends out a signal which may, with a relatively simple converter, be displayed on a standard TV set. The computer contains a mass storage area that the user reads by keying in the number of the "page" he wants: the computer keeps track of what pages the user looks at, and bills him accordingly. Prices for the pages are set by the information provider (IP), who rents the space from the system owner and receives the charges levied on the user for reading a page (less any service fee for system operating costs, data storage and the carrier's administrative and billing costs).

In principle, it is a relatively simple technical proposition to provide message facilities for videotext systems. There are, however, a number of problems. Terminals, while cheap, are of too low quality for general electronic mail service (EMS) application. Also, sharing of terminals between information access and EMS might be awkward; for example, where a secretary would do keying of mail, while the executive would need the information-access capability. Furthermore, to implement message facilities requires considerable extra investment by the PTT or carrier providing the videotext service — although such facilities (e.g., permitting access to the telex network) are likely to be provided in the longer term. For these and other reasons, it seems unlikely that videotext will offer a message system competitive with the EMS alternatives discussed in the rest of this book until the late 1980s, and we will not discuss them further.

COST AND PERFORMANCE PROJECTIONS FOR TRANSMISSION SERVICES

Although the technology of transmission is well developed, transmission systems, unlike terminals, are typically not owned by users. Thus while technological innovation is possible, even likely, it is outside of the control of the user. In this discussion we must consider, therefore, both the technological advances available and the actual implementation of them by carriers.

Transmission networks are configured to be suitable for the particular sort of traffic which predominates on them, and thus may be unsuitable for other purposes. The transmission speeds or billing practices designed for one use, for example, may be completely unacceptable for another. In addition, transmission networks generally represent substantial capital investment; hence, changes occur slowly or not at all, depending on user demand.

The projection of trends in transmission systems is also a much trickier business than projection of terminal trends, since the availability of service interacts with a host of regulatory, technical, policy and business trends. Nevertheless, a number of transmission networks currently available have application to electronic mail. We will examine these, as well as a number of services the carriers *could* adopt to provide superior electronic mail service.

The four basic network categories suitable for electronic mail are:

- voice

- message-switched

- telex

- data

Simple as this categorization may seem, there are several different types of voice and data networks to be considered, and a range of technological options for each. We will look at each in further detail.

Voice Networks

As we have already seen, current voice networks have a number of advantages for electronic mail use. First, the public switched telephone network (PSTN) is extensively developed and has substantial excess capacity in off-peak hours for electronic mail. In addition, everyone knows how to use it, and, perhaps most important, it is available now.

Disadvantages of Voice Network

However, there are considerable disadvantages associated with using the public telephone network for electronic mail service. First, it does not permit positive identification of a called terminal. Second, it requires end-to-end connections, something mail does not require. Instead, it is preferable that something analogous to the mail-slot or posting box should operate, so that a message is "dropped" into the system, and delivered in a reasonable period of time, freeing the operator to do other things and allowing him to ignore time-zone differences and "called-subscriber-busy" signals. Yet the present-day telephone network requires that the line at the other end be free at the time of sending, and that the connection be held open during the period of transmission. Similarly, a telephone system requires that the terminals at both ends be directly compatible. Also, billing practices usually set minimum calling periods, rarely less than 15 seconds, sometimes as much as three minutes, which would penalize electronic mail use, where text transmission may require only a couple of seconds per page, and facsimile less than a minute. Another potential problem is that where domestic mail charges are distance-independent, telephone charges vary as a function of distance.

Suggested Improvements

To a certain extent, these objections can be overcome by increasing the sophistication of terminals: store-and-forward capability can be provided by building in memory and automatic dialers. Additional usefulness would be provided by modification of the network itself — however, this can only be accomplished by the PTT or telephone company that operates it. Billing practices can be changed so that shorter calling periods are allowed, although there is a limit to this.* Store-and-forward could be provided in the network at prices below the cost of individual memory in terminals, both because the unit cost of storage drops as the size of a memory increases, and, perhaps more importantly, because a central location could make more efficient utilization of capacity than could the average user.

Store-and-forward capability

An advantage of store-and-forward to the carrier is that it allows "load levelling" to occur. Electronic mail messages would be sent only when excess capacity exists to handle it, and stored when capacity is saturated. This would also justify charging a lower rate than for a regular voice call, so that not only is convenience served, but also economy. Pricing would depend on the priori-

---

*It can be uneconomic to charge for very short periods (i.e., less than the relatively long time it takes to set up a telephone call) because charges may be billed only for connect time.

ty of service requested, with immediate (say 15-minute, guaranteed) delivery costing the most.

Another advantage of store-and-forward in the network is that it allows conversions between incompatible terminals. This is possible because messages must be stored, at which point it is relatively easy to translate them into any one of several standards before delivery. All the system needs to know are the characteristics of the sending and receiving terminals, which it can accomplish by "looking them up" in a directory, or by "interrogating" an intelligent terminal.

Broadcast features

Additionally, broadcast features can be provided. This allows a user to specify a number of addresses for a single message, which the system delivers to each automatically. Usually this feature also permits lists of addresses to be stored beforehand in the system, with the sender needing only to specify which list is to be used.

Digitization of the telephone network

The digitization of the telephone network (which is already occurring) offers the potential for very cheap electronic mail service, particularly when combined with store-and-forward. It turns out that on strict economic and technical grounds, the digital representation of the signals has advantages for voice transmission, and public telephone systems throughout the world are evolving toward increased use of digital technology. This means that data already in digital form could be transmitted directly on digital voice lines at much greater speed (see Figure 3.6). For example, a text terminal or Group 3 facsimile terminal produces digital information which is translated by a modem to an analog series of tones, and transmitted over telephone lines, which limits the transmission speed typically to 4800 bps. A digital telephone channel, however, samples and transmits a voice or other audio signal with a digital representation at a rate of 64,000 bps. Thus if the mass memory of a store-and-forward system were connected directly to a digital trunk, 64,000 bps transmission could be achieved at a cost no more than that of a regular phone line. Thus, what might take one minute to send over an analog telephone line, should take less than five seconds over a digital trunk, with a corresponding reduction in cost. A similar opportunity exists if special lines were supplied to users directly for their digital traffic. Together, this suggests that very low transmission costs indeed will be possible for electronic mail by the mid-1980s in many places.

Figure 3.6 Advantage of All-Digital Transmission for Digital Terminals

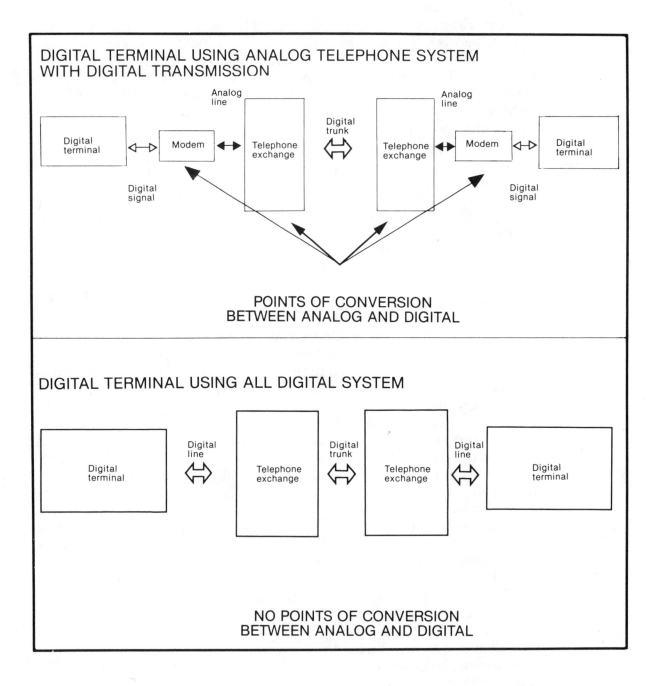

Telex Systems

Telex currently offers the advantage of a large and growing base of compatible terminals. Its disadvantages are many, however. It allows only low transmission rates and a restricted character set. Like the telephone it requires end-to-end connection, and since it is still true that most current types of telex terminals are engaged not only during message transmission but also during message preparation, call rejection rates are as high as 30% in peak periods. Moreover, most of the terminals in use are of old-fashioned design, and the noisy office environment they create is frequently a problem.

Suggested Improvements

A number of improvements in telex systems are likely to be widely implemented by the mid-1980s. New exchanges will allow store-and-forward, broadcasting (that is, the ability to send the same message to a large number of users at the same time) as well as abbreviated addressing, the ability to send a message to a preprogrammed address by using a short code. In addition, the advances in printing technology described earlier in this chapter are finding their way into telex terminals, resulting in quieter operation and better print quality. Telex, however, will still suffer from a restricted character set and slow printing speed which will limit its applicability for more general electronic mail use.

Message-Switched Systems

Message-switched systems have existed since the earliest days of telegraphy. They are, by definition, store-and-forward systems. A suitably addressed message is entered into the system without any end-to-end call connection being made, and therefore independently of whether the called station is free or busy.

The advantages of "message switches" are the same as for store-and-forward in the PSTN:

- Messages can be entered even if receiving terminal is busy;

- Incompatible terminals can communicate;

- Message broadcast is easily performed;

- Circuit utilization is more efficient.

The main disadvantage, and this also is true of store-and-forward in the PSTN, is that the originator of the message does not get an immediate answer-back, and must wait, perhaps until the next day, for confirmation of delivery. On the other hand, this act of faith is no more demanding than with any other mail service, and confirmation of delivery is cheaper and easier to provide than with conventional postal service.

An example of a message-switched system is ITT's COMTEL telex relay service, which is offered to subscribers in the U.K. It allows users to enter messages using any number or kind of terminals employing standard telephone, telex or data lines, and permits store-and-forward and broadcasting. The message is reformatted (if necesary) to telex format, and sent out over the telex network. Thus, in many ways it offers a prototype of the sort of electronic mail system we anticipate for the 1980s, but its restriction to telex limits its general applicability.

Data Networks

Data networks have developed primarily to serve the needs of computer users in a wide range of applications. They may offer circuit-switched or packet-switched, or dedicated leased line facilities. Generally, data networks share the following characteristics:

- High transmission speeds;

- Fast response times;

- Fast transit times through the network for short messages;

- Low error rates;

- Fast call set-up.

Also, the charges on some data networks, particularly packet-switched ones, are distance-independent.

Not all of these characteristics are necessarily desirable for electronic mail. Very high transmission speeds are often unnecessary, particularly for text transmission, unless there is a large volume of mail between terminals. Fast response and transit times are required by computer users for interactive time-sharing sessions or for transaction-oriented applications (e.g., in credit checking or reservations systems) where a wait of longer than a few seconds may be quite annoying to a user waiting at a terminal for a response, whereas for electronic mail a minimum transit time of even several minutes would almost always be acceptable. On the other hand, the characteristics of low error rates and distance-independent charges are extremely desirable for electronic mail.

Thus, while all data networks will not offer every user advantages over the telephone network, they may offer the best choice for many.

Circuit-switched Data Networks

Circuit-switched data networks, like the telephone and telex networks, require an end-to-end connection — that is, a free receiving terminal. But these networks may be very suitable for high-volume electronic mail traffic between limited numbers of sites, e.g., for bulk transfer of intraorganizational mail in a large corporation. Circuit-switched data networks can also be very suitable for high-speed facsimile traffic (i.e., large volumes of facsimile being transmitted at, say, 48,000 bps). If organizations already use circuit-switched data networks for data processing traffic, using the same networks for electronic mail may be attractive.

Packet-switched Data Networks

Packet-switched networks offer opportunities for lower volume electronic mail users. Conceptually, packet-switched networks are very much like message-switched networks, but designed for interactive computer use rather than conventional messages. (One difference is that a packet is of fixed size, and several may be required to send a message, while in a message-switched system, a packet is the whole message.) Each packet contains the address of the receiving terminal. The sending terminal inserts it into the network, where it is sent to the first switching point. There the address is read, and the packet held until a line is open to the next switching point along the way, to which the packet is then sent. There the process continues, until eventually the packet reaches the destination terminal. Thus, at no point is a complete circuit required, making packet-switching extremely economical for sending relatively small amounts of information long distances.*

---

*Circuit-switching is more economical for sending large amounts of information, since a certain amount of processing is required at each decision point along a packet-switched network. For small amounts of information, this is much less than the cost of setting up and holding a circuit. For example, an international circuit might take a minute to set up, and be used for only a fraction of a second.

Packet-switched vs. Message-switched Networks

There is a major, functional difference between message-switched and packet-switched networks, however. Packet-switched systems only have enough storage within the network to hold individual packets for very short periods at a time (small fractions of a second). A message-switched network has far greater storage capacity, and may store complete messages for minutes or more.

There are further disadvantages with most packet-switched networks currently in use. One is that the fast transit time designed into the network is usually unnecessary for mail traffic. This means that transmission costs more than it would if the system had been designed so that mail packets could travel at a lower priority than packets for transactions or other interactive applications. Another drawback is that most packet sizes presently in use (or proposed) are generally too small for electronic mail messages. This means that messages, particularly digital facsimile, require a large number of packets — with all of the extra overhead that this entails. Therefore electronic mail sent over packet-switched networks will cost somewhat more than should optimally be necessary.

Suggested Improvements

All of these technical problems can be solved if the designers of the system take the trouble to solve them, and computer experts say this will not be difficult. For example, networks could be organized so that electronic mail messages labelled "second class" travel during off-peak times, and thus do not clog the network when more urgent communication is in progress. If system operators want to attract electronic mail traffic, they should be motivated to make both the technical and economic changes required for this. The advantage of a packet-switched system, if properly designed for electronic mail application, is the extreme economy of use, particularly since both computer users and electronic mail users will share the same network and its costs.

SUMMARY

As we have seen, all of the transmission networks discussed have potential for electronic mail use. Some may suit high volume users better than low volume users, and vice versa.

We can see from the discussion, however, that in the worst case, the cost and difficulty of sending a page of electronic mail should be less than a one minute phone call for Group 3 facsimile, and much less for a page of text. Store-and-forward, technically feasible in a number of systems from the phone system to data networks, offers both the possibility of increased convenience and substantial reductions in cost, so that costs per page on the order of one tenth to one twentieth of the cost of a one minute telephone call are not unreasonable.

The critical factor is how fast these features will become available in the near future, a question to which we will return in the next section.

Section II: Electronic Mail and Your Business

- ☑ **Why Electronic Mail?**

- ☑ **Choosing the Best System for Your Organization**

- ☑ **Evaluating Single Purpose vs. Multipurpose Systems**

- ☑ **Evaluating Transmission Speed vs. Terminal Cost**

- ☑ **Evaluating Print and Display Quality**

- ☑ **Security and Privacy Issues**

- ☑ **Compatibility**

- ☑ **Analyzing Your Basic Requirements**

- ☑ **Survey Techniques for Determining Mail Flows**

- ☑ **Identifying the Critical Uses and Users of Electronic Mail**

- ☑ **Making the Transition to Electronic Mail**

4

Why Electronic Mail?

This is the first chapter that will deal concretely with the individual problems faced by organizations making the transition to electronic mail. Of course, the most immediate question is why make the transition at all? The answer is the concern of this chapter, and will be based on two simple ideas: that electronic mail is cheaper than its conventional alternatives and that it is better. Of course, the two arguments are related — at any point in the discussion of price we must ask, "For what quality of service?", and in the analysis of service we must ask, "For what price?"

ELECTRONIC MAIL WILL BE CHEAPER

The cost of mail includes both direct and indirect elements. On the one hand are such direct requirements as labor, paper and postage; on the other are less obvious elements like the cost of filing, of maintaining a mailing list or of copying and distributing correspondence internally. In addition, there are the hidden costs of contracts lost due to slow delivery; of duplicated work because information at another office cannot be received in time; of slow payments ("Your check is in the mail") or of misunderstandings caused by letters crossing in the mail.

Price Trends for Conventional Mail Service

Figure 4.1 charts the trend in the retail price index for key components of conventional mail service in the U.S. from 1975 to 1980. During this time, the cost of a first-class letter rose 50%, from 10 cents to 15 cents, while third-class and parcel post rates advanced 35% and 42.8%. The cost of paper was up 45%. By 1982, first-class postage was up to 20 cents.

The same trends are at work in other countries, often to a greater extent. Thus, Figure 4.2 reproduces the retail price index for the U.K. of the direct component costs of mail: we see that the cost of secretarial labor has been increasing at a compound interest rate of over 15%. The cost of stationery goods has increased by 15% as well, and postage by over 20% annually.

Figure 4.1 U.S. Price Index for Conventional Postal Service Items, 1975-1980

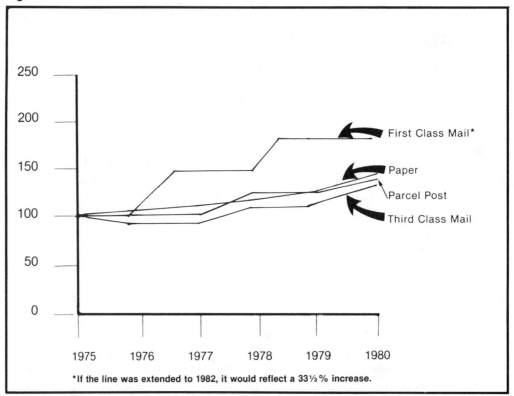

*If the line was extended to 1982, it would reflect a 33⅓% increase.

Source: U.S. Postal Service: United Parcel Service; *Statistical Abstract of the United States, 1980*, U.S. Dept. of Commerce, Bureau of the Census.

These trends can only continue in the foreseeable future. Demand for paper products shows no signs of abating, while production capacity is difficult to increase, and the prices of substitutes — for example plastics — are increasing even faster because of their dependence on oil. Secretarial labor is in short supply, and market forces may keep wages climbing faster than inflation. The postal service, a labor intensive industry, will also undoubtedly have to continue to increase its prices faster than the rate of inflation.

The trends in electronic mail are exactly the opposite. While some correspondence will always be paper-based, electronic mail offers the opportunity to reduce the amount of paper used. Routine messages can be displayed on CRTs, with printing reserved only for items which have specific need for it. Transmission by electronic means is generally completely automated, and, as we have seen, its technology is continuing to improve. Finally, the intelligence of electronic mail terminals, most particularly of word processors, allows secretarial productivity to increase, while the capital cost of these systems, as we saw in the last chapter, is falling rapidly.

Figure 4.2 U.K. Retail Price Index for Post, Secretarial Labor, and Stationery Goods, 1975-1979 (1975 = 100)

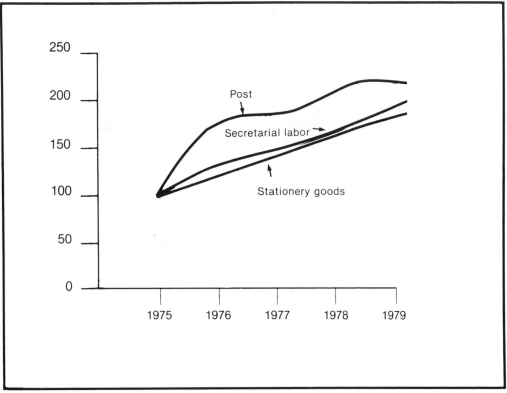

Source: Mackintosh International and Communications Studies and Planning Ltd., 1978.

Deterioration of Conventional Mail Service

A further trend, related to the rising cost of postal service, has been a steady deterioration in the quality of first-class mail. In the United States, for example, where overnight delivery used to be standard for intra-city delivery and between major city centers, two- to three-day delivery is now a more realistic standard and the degree of uncertainty about what the delay will be in any particular case has also increased. Similar patterns have been found in Canada, France and West Germany. In West Germany, for example, over half of the firms interviewed expressed dissatisfaction with the delivery speed of regular post.

Alternative Delivery Services

The need for rapid delivery has spawned a significant business in alternative delivery services, which can demand large premiums over regular post. In the

United States, for example, Express Mail guarantees overnight delivery between most major cities in the continental United States at a price about 30 times that for a one-ounce letter. Second day delivery between New York and London costs about 60 times as much as an airmail letter. In the U.K., the Post Office offers its Datapost service at similar premiums, as do the authorities in Germany, France and Canada. In addition, particularly in the United States, private airfreight and courier companies offer a wide variety of premium mail services.

If we accept the charge for a one minute telephone call as an upper limit on the cost of transmitting a single page of electronic mail, we see that electronic means are already more than competitive with these special services. The average charge for a one minute long-distance call in the United States is about $.40, about one tenth the cost of Express Mail; a direct-dialed international call from London to New York is about $1.85 (£0.87), about one fourteenth of the corresponding rate for next-day physical delivery, £12 ($25.56).

In fact, electronic mail transmitted over the telephone is already competitive with international telex for long messages. Compare, for example, Group 3 facsimile with telex. A telex message costing no more than a telephone call between New York and London may contain only about 50 words, while a standard size page, single-spaced in 10 point type, containing 700 words can be sent via facsimile for the same cost. A modern communicating word processor has an even greater advantage.

ELECTRONIC MAIL WILL BE BETTER

As first outlined, therefore, electronic mail, even without any improvements in transmission systems, is already competitive with specialized delivery services. An additional feature is, of course, that the service is actually better since delivery can be instantaneous. In more developed forms, using store-and-forward and the telephone network, electronic mail could offer routine same day or overnight delivery at costs no greater than for first-class mail.

Improved Productivity

In addition to improvements in delivery speed, electronic mail offers the opportunity for improvements in the productivity of work generated by correspondence. A major consideration is that electronic mail items may be processed by computers. Thus, for example, an order received in a standard text format can be directly transferred to an accounting computer without having to be re-keyed. A letter received electronically can be filed electronically in a computer-indexed memory bank. Memoranda prepared on a communicating word processor can be distributed electronically according to pre-programmed mailing lists — so that a few keywords specify "every manager above Grade 4 with line responsibilities for personnel management" or any other arbitrarily complex combination of variables.

Integrated Office Communication Systems

Clearly all of these examples, typical of the sort of actions which are required by correspondence, demand a great deal of labor and expense in the absence of electronic aid. Yet all can be incorporated into an integrated office communications system of which electronic mail is a part.

This convergence of electronic mail with other office activities is one of the ways that the major objection to electronic mail, its high start-up cost, is overcome. Many organizations have already invested in systems — word processing, data processing, private automatic telephone exchanges (PABXs) — which provide the basic building blocks of an electronic mail system. For most of these organizations, the advantages of electronic mail might not by themselves justify the cost of building a system from scratch, but can be more easily justified as a relatively low cost addition to current expenditures.

For example, many organizations have invested in stand-alone word processors, simply on the basis of improved typing efficiency. Most stand-alone units currently do not provide communications capability as a standard option, but, as we have seen, this should be common practice by the early 1980s. Thus, organizations that would invest in word processing anyway will find that for an additional $10 or $20 a month they can own an electronic mail terminal.

A similar phenomenon is occurring in business data processing systems. Many small business computers now provide a text editing system as a standard feature or as a low-cost option. As processors are becoming cheaper and faster, these computers easily have enough power to provide all business data processing requirements as well as to drive one or more word processing terminals. Very often these systems are connected to telecommunications lines for data transmission purposes. Thus, these users have the basis of a very powerful electronic mail system for little more than the cost of one or two terminals and, perhaps, a high quality printer. They also benefit from the ability to merge information provided by correspondence directly with data processing; for example, in order handling.

SUMMARY

In summary, the answer to the question, ''Why electronic mail?'' contains several arguments.

Electronic mail is cheaper:

- in comparison to premium delivery services;

- in comparison even to first-class post, if advanced transmission systems are provided;

- in utilization of labor and materials.

Electronic mail is better:

- because it provides quicker delivery than cost-equivalent traditional services;

- because it integrates easily into computer-assisted communications, filing and data processing systems.

In addition, the start-up costs of electronic mail can be reduced substantially because very often many of the elements are already present, and cost-justified by other uses.

5

Fundamentals of System Design

CHOOSING THE BEST SYSTEM FOR YOUR ORGANIZATION

As was seen in the last chapter, considerations of cost and quality of service are inseparable. To many potential users, electronic mail provides the opportunity for better service than they currently receive at little or no additional cost. However, to many others, electronic mail offers the possibility of *much* better service at additional cost, or reduced service at lower cost than is possible using conventional means.

The individual factors that affect this analysis are numerous; it is important to consider the complexity of these factors and how they relate to user needs. In this chapter we will examine a number of factors, including:

- print quality
- transmission speed
- terminal cost
- security and privacy
- convenience
- compatibility.

As with terminal design, where better performance must be paid for, we note here that the process of system design is one of balancing requirements with costs. This chapter will illustrate the dimensions which can shift the balance in favor of one application or another, but the value of this shift can be determined only by the individual user.

CASE STUDIES IN ELECTRONIC MAIL USE

Perhaps the best way to illustrate this balancing process is to describe a number of organizations that already incorporate electronic mail into their daily work. Of course, no organization today can use electronic mail to handle all of its written communications with the outside world, simply because the use of electronic mail is not sufficiently widespread.* Nevertheless, even with this limitation, many organizations have found the adoption of electronic mail useful, and their experience will illustrate many of the factors affecting system design.

The case studies that follow are derived from more than 200 in-depth, personal interviews conducted in the course of preparing this report.

Case Study: A Multinational Oil Company

This major multinational oil company, based on the West Coast of the United States, is using a combination of TWX machines, facsimile, communicating word processors and conventional postal service for urgent message traffic. Three TWX units receive 18,000 and send 12,000 messages a year, while a machine used for international traffic handles 16,000 messages. Two facsimile machines at headquarters are in communication with 60 other fax units scattered throughout the company; annual traffic is 29,000 messages. Facsimile is heavily used to send legal documents back and forth between headquarters and Washington, DC.

System Features

A Hewlett-Packard 3000 minicomputer at headquarters is used for word processing and other functions; it supports 50 terminals in all, of which 20 are used for word processing. People can address messages to colleagues, storing them in the host computer; recipients check their "mail box" by logging in at a word processing terminal. One intriguing project involves extending the electronic mail network to Chicago, using a microwave link. In general, such a link would not be economical, but the company already owns the microwave channel, and is looking for ways to add traffic. The microwave network provides high-speed (9.6 kilobit) links as well as slower (4.8 kilobit) lines to three major cities. Total telecommunications service costs amount to $5 million per year. Both the telecommunications and data processing departments report to a corporate information services center, whereas the office services department reports to the corporate secretary.

---

*The nature of a communications network is such that the more people there are who can use it, the more valuable it is.

Future Plans

The company has ambitious plans to upgrade its telecommunications network, by adding the capability to handle high speed facsimile and video conferencing, as well as expanded electronic mail. The timetable in word processing and electronic mail is first to automate the secretarial aspects of text preparation, then to look at work stations that can access information stored in a central data base.

Case Study 2: An International Bank

This international bank, based in New York, employs 18,000 people in 250 locations around the world, most of them in branches with fewer than 100 people. There are seven offices employing at least 200 people; the headquarters staff consists of 3000 employees, 2000 managers and 1000 clerks and secretaries.

Extensive data processing and data communications facilities support the bank's domestic and international communications. For example, there are three telex switching centers — in New York, London and Hong Kong — and New York traffic alone runs 6000 messages a day. Most of these deal with funds transfer. Two hundred TWX machines are used for domestic money transfers.

System Features

Thirty-five branches have fax transceivers, and 10 machines are located in the bank's money transfer center. Two voice-grade dedicated lines to London carry fax traffic in off hours.

Among the bank's 10 different data networks are ones dedicated to savings, retail applications, commercial loans, etc. Some 1200 terminals are connected online to these data networks, of which 500 terminals are in the branches. Computer equipment includes five mainframe IBM computers, 12 NCR computers and about 130 minicomputers. The bank spends $20 million a year on computer rental, and $15 to $20 million on communications. There are also 300 word processors in place.

The bank has moved toward the virtual elimination of conventional postal service for communication between various branches. If messages can't be sent by telex, TWX, facsimile or online computer terminal, they are often sent by courier, including courier to overseas locations. In establishing advanced office systems for internal electronic mail, the bank would handle security and privacy by requiring passwords of the sort used in computer timesharing systems.

Case Study 3: An Insurance Company

This insurance company operates mostly within West Germany, and consists of a headquarters and a number of branch offices. Currently, the company uses electronic mail in two forms: first, it sends about 400 and receives 400 telex messages each month, mostly communicating insurance and technical information between itself and major customers; second, it has converted most of its transaction communications to a computer-based system. These transaction items (accounts, statements, etc.) are processed by a central computer in headquarters linked by private circuits to terminals in subsidiary establishments.

Employees participated in designing the transaction system, and it was introduced after internal training programs. Despite initial employee skepticism, since 1974 the system has reduced costs and diverted an estimated 80% of transaction mail from postal services. The company would be prepared to convert more of its postal and telex messages to other forms of electronic mail.

Case Study 4: A Multinational Engineering Firm

This firm has 11 main locations in five countries. At its principal European site it has roughly 900 staff of whom 200 are office workers and the remainder are technicians or engineers.

System Features

The company is served by several electronic mail systems. Sixteen telex terminals distributed among the 11 locations handle about 100 messages per day. (Fourteen of these terminals are part of a private telex network among the various branches.) The organization is a very heavy user of data processing, and therefore operates a complex data network linking the computers at its various sites with 9600 bps leased circuits; these are shared by facsimile terminals. Facsimile volumes are about 1300 pages a month within the organization and about 18 pages per month to or from other organizations.

One factor encouraging use of facsimile by this company is the need to send drawings and technical information. Another was the decision to use the high-speed telecommunications circuits employed for data communications, for facsimile traffic.

The facsimile system is considered a success by management: it has reduced postal and telex traffic and provides greater efficiency and faster communications. Although no cost reductions have been achieved, the advantages of better and faster communications are thought to outweigh the additional cost.

Future Plans

The company would like to expand its use of electronic alternatives to the mails. The prime considerations would be the cost, flexibility and quality of the service, and its ability to send "signed" documents. Any new electronic message service would probably use packet-switched facilities, if available.

One problem in developing future services is how to manage the overlap between telecommunications, data processing and office equipment. The company sees the desirability of combining these functions within a single department, but as yet, managers with the necessary breadth of skills are not available.

Case Study 5: An International Office Equipment/High Technology Manufacturer

System Features

This manufacturer has telex units at 22 locations domestically and 106 teletype machines linked by private wire in the U.S., plus 71 machines in Europe on a similar switched, private network. The company also leases 20 private-line teletype circuits to Europe. Telex is used for general administrative messages, internal orders and incoming customer orders. The U.S. headquarters in the Midwest handles 7000 domestic telex messages out and 10,000 messages in per month, and a total of 4000 international messages.

The company also has 300 facsimile units in the U.S. and 200 abroad; in the U.S. the volume of traffic is 5000 to 10,000 documents a month, consisting of administrative messages and some outside purchase orders and specifications.

Future Plans

The company is in the process of an ambitious commitment to word processors that can serve as the basis for an expanded electronic mail service. The proposed system would use word processing, fax, intelligent copiers and optical character recognition, and the result would be to replace the domestic telex network. The electronic mail service will stress intracompany communications; studies show that they could send an 1800-character message for 19 cents electronically.

The postal service is most important to billing and collections at present, with urgent company messages already sent via telex, not mail. The annual postal bill (excluding billing or advertising) is about $1 million, compared with $2 million spent on courier services. The word processing/electronic mail network is expected to replace 40% to 50% of the present cost of couriers.

Case Study 6: An Overseas Bank

This major Italian bank says it has eliminated use of the postal service for internal communication, although it still uses the mails for messages to and from other organizations. Its communication with branches around the country employs:

- telex support by a message switch at headquarters;

- facsimile — for signature verification;

- SWIFT, an international banking message system;

- a real-time transaction processing system whereby tellers' terminals are linked via leased circuits to a computer at headquarters;

- a private fleet of vehicles which provides overnight service to all branches in mainland Italy — though not to outside organizations.

Introduction of the bank's real-time system and of SWIFT required considerable training, which the bank regards as successful: staff with no experience on terminals were persuaded to operate the new equipment, at no increase in pay (the unions did demand such increases). Productivity of the tellers is much improved. The bank plans to double the number of tellers' terminals in the next three to five years, and also to increase its usage of SWIFT as more banks come on the system.

The well-publicized problems of the postal service in Italy have obviously contributed to this company's development of electronic alternatives. The reasons for not using the mails are its slow speed and less than total reliability. Security is another factor in the expanding use of electronic services.

Case Study 7: A Major Computer Manufacturer

This rapidly growing major manufacturer of minicomputers, located in New England, has been operating its own internal electronic mail system since the late 1970s. By 1981, 3500 managers, professionals and assistants had passwords authorizing them to use the system, which consists of eight "nodes," each with its own central processor and disc drives, and each connected to terminals accessible to users.

System Features

According to the company's manager of corporate message services, volume on the network is running at the rate of 9000 messages delivered daily. About one in three users has direct access to a computer terminal for using the service and one in five has a terminal at home. One of the most important features of the service is a central directory of names and addresses, permitting any user to quickly identify another person to whom he wants to send a message.

Short memos relating to every sort of company operations are the brunt of the traffic. "It has definitely speeded up the metabolism of the organization," says the director of the system. "It beats 'telephone tag' " for delivering brief messages, he says. Field consultants and outside salespeople use the system as a prime means of contact with colleagues.

The EMS system connects to the company's message-switched network using conventional TWX and telex for printed record communications; the company has 600 TWX and telex terminals in the U.S., and 50 abroad, with traffic running at 12,000 messages per day. By the late 1970s, the company was spending $25 million on communications, and $15 million on mail services.

Demand for access to the EMS system thus far exceeds the capacity of the system, and one concern is that storage at each node — consisting of four disc drives containing 400 million characters of capacity — will run out unless users regularly purge the system of unwanted information. (Records management is emerging as a significant problem, the company notes.) Users are charged the cost of using the service, but hardware costs are much lower than for an outside organization, because the company manufactures its own terminals and central processing units. Costs of operating the system consist of 1) personnel to run each node; 2) hardware (CPU and disc drives) at each node; 3) user terminals; and 4) communications costs. If a company had to install such a system and pay going market prices for the equipment, the manager says, the tab would come to about $80 per user per month.

Future Plans

The company is not able to say if any conventional paper-based mail has been displaced by the system; it's even possible that such mail has increased, the director says, since EMS seems to stimulate the quantity of communication, as well as improving the quality. There are no plans to open the network for messages to and from outside organizations, one concern being to protect the security of internal communications.

These seven firms represent a wide range of needs and uses, from the insurance company and banks with a large demand for transaction-based correspondence, to the engineering firm with a high degree of technical correspondence, to the two manufacturing firms and oil company, which might be seen as somewhere in between the others. All have made substantial investment in electronic mail which has been justified in different ways by the different kinds of organizations.

We turn now to the various elements of the design process in somewhat more formal terms.

EVALUATING SINGLE PURPOSE VS. MULTIPURPOSE SYSTEMS

All the case studies illustrate this issue to some extent. The insurance company needed a computer to process its transactions anyway; it found it useful to set up a data network and provide terminals so that the transaction could be transmitted electronically instead of through the mail. The engineering firm already had a data network in place because it was a heavy user of computers; it was economical to provide facsimile terminals that would share the data network, rather than use the telephone. The office equipment manufacturer maintained two sets of terminals — telex and teletype terminals and stand-alone word processors. It found that it could eliminate the telex and teletype terminals by adopting a standard communicating word processor which could link, when necessary, to these networks. The computer manufacturer had the great advantage of making most of the equipment used in its system, thus reducing costs considerably.

In general then, comparisons between single and multipurpose machines must go deeper than just a look at the price tag. As the examples show, a communicating word processor costs more than a noncommunicating word processor, but it may eliminate the need for other terminals; a higher capacity data transmission system may cost more than a lower capacity one, but may allow the addition of electronic mail.

EVALUATING TRANSMISSION SPEED VS. TERMINAL COST

Here the trade-off is not quite as simple as it looks. In general, a less expensive terminal will operate more slowly but, since transmission charges are a function of time, will cost more to operate. The primary example is the difference between the various groups of facsimile machines. Group 2 machines, transmitting a page in less than three minutes, are typically more cost-effective (even for very low usage) than cheaper Group 1 machines which require up to six minutes per page.

Transmission Charges

In other cases, however, the basis of charging for transmission, particularly in the telephone networks, can make it difficult to evaluate the economics of higher transmission speeds. The factor of relevance here is the minimum charging period adopted by the carrier. For if the minimum charge for a domestic call allows for, say, 30 seconds of time, then there is no advantage in increasing the transmission rate beyond what would give a transmission time of less than 30 seconds. But if the minimum charging period for international calls is only two or three seconds,* increased transmission speeds may be attractive. Thus, in an economic analysis, the distance and type of call must be considered.

Transmission Rates

For communicating word processor traffic, it is possible that a transmission rate higher than 2400 bps (about one single-spaced page in 20 seconds) will not be necessary. But for facsimile traffic, transmission even at 9600 bps requires up to 20 seconds per page, and in many countries, transmission at this speed is not possible. (Most modern digital facsimile terminals will incorporate intelligent modems which will operate as fast as line quality will allow, and will drop to slower speeds if line quality deteriorates.)

---

*This is true in the U.K. and much of Europe, but not in the U.S., where the minimum international call is generally one minute.

Volume of Mail

Within these limits the volume of electronic mail to be transmitted is a major determining factor in selecting terminal equipment. The choice should go to the terminal that minimizes the average cost per message, including the cost (per month) of the terminal and special transmission lines (if any) divided by the average number of messages per month. In this way, the fixed monthly cost of renting equipment is seen as a proportion of each message's cost.

EVALUATING PRINT AND DISPLAY QUALITY

Here again the principle is that better performance must be paid for. The case studies illustrate this.

Consider the office equipment manufacturer. Conversion to communicating word processors was expected to divert 40% to 50% of traffic away from courier services to electronic transmission. Why, when a private teletype network already existed? Partially because communicating word processors offer a larger character-set and better print quality than do teletypes, allowing traffic to be diverted to the word processors. Another reason is that communicating word processors eliminate the need to rekey already typewritten messages.

Thus, if an organization has a large number of items which require rapid transmission and high print quality, then a terminal that fails to provide high quality is not satisfactory. On the other hand, for transactions, a company like the insurance company has a need for legibility only and a lower quality terminal is perfectly adequate.

In display a similar process operates, although its effect may be more subtle. One consideration is operator fatigue — a low quality screen is unpleasant to look at and tiring. The effect could be to reduce typing efficiency. Also, if users find the display unpleasant to look at, they will print more items than would otherwise be necessary, thus wasting paper.

The size of the display may be another consideration. A large display will allow a whole page to be displayed at once. While there is some controversy over whether whole page displays increase typing efficiency, they are essential for formatting and editing complex documents without creating a paper copy.

EVALUATING CENTRALIZED VS. DISTRIBUTED SYSTEMS

Centralized systems very often have price and performance advantages over distributed systems. Usually this is the result of the sharing of a single, powerful piece of equipment by several work stations — say a high speed electrostatic printer — and the elimination of separate, less powerful units at each station (in this example, by eliminating the need for individual printers and relying on the CRT displays alone).

Centralization is not a panacea, however, and a number of factors must be considered before designing a centralized system. Before discussing these it is useful to draw a distinction between centralization of *hardware,* and centralization of *function.* Centralization of hardware implies, simply, that a job which could be performed by several small machines is instead performed by fewer, large ones. Centralization of function implies specialization.

The introduction of electronic mail, along with the word processing and electronic filing that will often accompany it, presents the system designer with a wealth of possibilities for centralizing or not, as he chooses. The factors affecting his decision will differ, in each case, depending on whether he is centralizing hardware or function. In the first case he is dealing with the characteristics of hardware; in the second, with the human factors which affect hardware and performance. While centralization of function and hardware sometimes overlap, they are quite distinct. For example, as seen in Case Study 7, a central computer system can provide a powerful, general purpose communications system throughout the organization.

Centralizing Hardware

The decision to centralize hardware is generally a trade-off between cost and convenience, and to a lesser extent, reliability and security.

One decision is whether to purchase a system in which a single processor drives a number of work stations, or in which each work station has its own processor. It turns out that the cost of processors has declined to the point that, for newly produced systems, there is much less cost advantage in centralizing processing. However, many of the more powerful word processing systems currently on the market were designed around a single, central processor. Their development costs have been paid for, and often they have provided a more attractive operator environment, with plain English commands and more powerful and flexible file-handling and indexing, than many current distributed (stand-alone) systems. Currently, they may cost no more than two or three correspondingly powerful stand-alone units, and this may be attractive to some users.

Advantages of Centralization

Centralization of printing and electronic filing can offer considerable price and performance advantages over their distributed alternatives. A single electrostatic printer could replace dozens of daisy-wheel or matrix line printers, at lower cost. It would offer better print quality than a matrix printer, and full graphics capability (which neither of the other two offers) along with the opportunity to print, for example, large numbers of personalized letters for bulk mailings.

Disadvantages of Centralization

These advantages must be measured against a number of disadvantages. The first is reliability. If the single electrostatic printer breaks down, the printing function for the entire office is crippled, whereas if the printing is distributed, only a limited number of users are affected, and their load can be taken up by the printers that are still functioning. This consideration applies generally to all sorts of hardware centralization.

Another consideration is the risk of creating bottlenecks. If one person is printing for a mass mailing, someone else who needs a few pages printed urgently may find it impossible. This drawback, too, applies to any equipment used by a number of people.

A final consideration is the sheer convenience of having a number of printers at different locations — if not at every work station, then at least one convenient to each. In an organization spread out over a large area, simply distributing the output from a single printing location may waste a great deal of personnel time.

Other Considerations

Centralization of peripheral memory is another option open to the designer. Here again, reliability is an important factor. Another consideration is that different users sharing, say, the same disc drive, might require different discs to be mounted. Thus, centralized filing requires greater coordination, and, in addition, may often require an operator at a remote location to change files and otherwise work the system. On the other hand, centralization and coordination of filing means that more users will have access to files which, in a distributed system, would be inaccessible. Duplication is thus reduced. Inevitably, however, this increases the risk of unauthorized use or inadvertent erasure of files. Some of these problems can be mitigated, however, by providing each typist with his or her own small tape or disc drive for active files, and by providing a central file with strict security for archival storage.

Centralization vs. Distribution of Function

Introduction of electronic mail and particularly, word processing, is very often seen as an opportunity to better coordinate office activity. Indeed, when well thought out, it can lead to marked improvement in productivity. However, one inherent danger in the introduction of a new technology is that it often requires other changes in office functions which are not provided for ahead of time, and may be counterproductive.

One common change associated with word processing is the transformation of secretarial jobs from general purpose ones, including typing, to more specific ones with word processing as a separate, specialized skill. This may occur simply because there is money to purchase only a single word processor, and only one secretary is trained to use it, whereas demand for word processing may come from all of the executives in the office. The secretary trained on the word processor may then have to devote most of her time to typing and less to other tasks, and may not feel that this is an improvement in the quality of her work.

In addition, as with centralization of hardware, centralizing function risks creating bottlenecks. If an organization is committed to centralized word processing or electronic mail, it may be very difficult to "farm out" overloads to other secretaries within the organization. On the other hand, if functions are kept distributed, overloads in one area can be handled more easily.

As the price of electronic mail and word processing terminals drops, it is likely that the flexibility offered by distributed systems will outweigh some of the cost advantages now held by centralized systems. For example, when the cost of a word processor is only fractionally more than a standard office typewriter, every secretary can have one, and the system designer will have greater freedom to choose the ideal design from a human factors standpoint.

SECURITY AND PRIVACY ISSUES

Security and privacy problems with electronic mail are probably no more severe than with conventional mail.* What is clear, however, is that they are different and require, from the perspective of users experienced only with physical transmission systems, novel solutions.

One problem is that electronic mail items generally do not arrive in envelopes. While electronic safeguards offering far more security than an envelope are workable, in practice few letters really need this. Rather, adequate planning on the part of electronic mail system designers should be enough. In general, for example, printers should not be located in public areas, but at either individual secretaries' desks, or in a private area with restricted access.

A potentially more serious security problem is the possibility of electronic interception of electronic mail items, for example by tapping telephone lines. In fact it may be easier for a skilled and determined spy to intercept an electronic letter than a conventional one. However, for very sensitive material, encryption can provide for very secure transmission. Thus, compared to physical transmission, where a determined spy can also intercept items, the risks of electronic mail seem acceptable.

COMPATIBILITY

A further consideration in designing an electronic mail system is compatibility; that is, the ability of one terminal to communicate with others. Here again a number of options are open to the system designer.

Importance of Standardization

Currently, electronic mail standards are set by individual companies. Thus, several manufacturers will market different products which will be incompatible. Sometimes the market leader gains an advantage when his market lead becomes a selling point. ("Buy my terminal because you can reach more people than with my competitor's.") Because of this, other manufacturers may redesign their products to be compatible with the leader. (Of course these problems may be mitigated by intelligent networks.)

---

*An exception to this generalization exists when electronic mail is combined with computer archiving and storage. In the worst case, this means that breaches of security can occur more suddenly and be more severe — simply because of the ease with which large amounts of information can be transferred.

This is not always an orderly process. Often different standards can coexist for a long period of time, especially if one standard has advantages for some uses, and another has advantages for others. However, because of the characteristic of a communications network that the more people who are accessible on it and whose addresses are known, the more valuable it is to all, the adoption of universal standards is generally welcome.

There are two restrictions on this generalization. First, if the primary use is internal, it is only necessary that all of the terminals within an organization be compatible. This risks, however, being unable to expand the system if no consideration is given to outside compatibility. For example, in designing a text system based on communicating word processors, different sites might have different requirements. Headquarters might need a large, shared-processing system, while a branch office might need only a single, stand-alone processor. The problem is to find stand-alone and shared processing systems that are compatible with each other. The other consideration is that intelligent networks might be available that will accomplish conversion between a number of different terminal types. Then the problem is to ensure that all of the terminals purchased are accommodated by the network,* and that all potential addressees can be reached.

Text Terminals

The major factors affecting the compatibility of text terminals are:

- The character set. For example, do they have upper and lower case letters, or upper case only?

- The coding of characters. Two terminals may have the same alphabet, but if they encode them differently for transmission they will be incompatible.

- The control codes. How does the terminal signal, for example, the start of a new page or that the message is over?

Facsimile Terminals

Similarly, for facsimile terminals, important variables are:

---

*Often manufacturers never formally agree on a standard between themselves, but the adoption of a standard by the carrier creates the standard.

- The scanning density. How many scanning lines to the page? How large are the individual dots which are encoded?

- Compression algorithm. For example, does the facsimile terminal skip white lines? If so, how is this signalled?

In addition to all of the considerations for both facsimile and text, combined text and graphics terminals must also have a way of knowing when to shift from one mode to another.

Other Considerations

General considerations for all kinds of terminals include:

- Paper size and handling conventions. A multi-page message cannot be received if the terminal can handle only a single page. Similarly, if pages are of different size, a message sent from one terminal may not fit onto the page of another.

- Store-and-forward conventions. How should messages be formatted? How should multiple addresses or different priorities be specified?

- Communications protocols. The technical aspects of signalling which allow terminals to talk to one another.

A final consideration is the provision of directories. Directories are needed to know what establishments are equipped for electronic mail, what kind of messages they can receive and how they can be reached.

Standards-setting Bodies

In addition to informal, or *de facto,* means of setting standards, two formal bodies have responsibility in this area. One is the International Standards Organization (ISO); the other is the International Telephone and Telegraph Consultative Committee (CCITT) which is part of the International Telecommunication Union (a specialized agency of the United Nations) and is directly responsible for setting standards for international telephone, telegraph and other telecommunications media. A number of issues of relevance to electronic mail are currently under consideration by the CCITT.

The CCITT has already set some standards for facsimile systems, such as those for the Group 1 and 2 terminals already described, and is in the process of studying others. These include parameter conversion between different standards, as well as standards for store-and-forward and multi-address calling. It is also working on the "Teletex" standard described below.

The Teletex Standard

The basic idea behind the Teletex proposals was to develop a more powerful telex service, offering higher transmission rates, wider character sets and other desirable features — but the implications are now much broader. Now in fact the introduction of the Teletex standard is probably the single most important factor, particularly in Europe, contributing to the potential growth of electronic mail. Although final details have not been announced, the standard provides for most of the minimum requirements for a fully developed electronic mail system, and could form the basis for a communicating word processor standard.

The origin of the Teletex standard can be traced to the report of a government-appointed commission on telecommunications policy in the Federal Republic of Germany in 1976 (the so-called KtK report).

The basic tenets upon which the standard is being developed are:

- International compatibility;

- Full automatic message transfer for both the network and terminals;

- Large character repertoire;

- Transmission controls and protocols capable of allowing

    1) private special functions
    2) national and private alphabets in addition to the international standard alphabet
    3) compatibility with facsimile for graphic inserts into text or text reception by a facsimile terminal;

- Editing and other text manipulation facilities;

- Reception and transmission while the terminal is in the local mode (i.e., editing or text preparation);

- Specified minimum performance as far as error rates and availability are concerned;

- Minimum transmission rates for international use.

Thus, if fully implemented, Teletex could be the basis of a general-purpose, electronic mail system for communicating word processors.

Special Consideration for Users in the United States, Canada and Europe

To a great extent, the problems of compatibility depend on the regulatory environment of the country in which an installation is contemplated. In some, the operator of the telecommunications service is, by law, able to restrict severely the kinds of terminal devices that may be attached to the network. In other countries, a user may attach virtually any device as long as it meets minimal technical standards designed to keep it from damaging the network.

Most European countries are clearly in the first category, the only partial exception (following a recent ruling by the Monopolies Commission) being the Federal Republic of Germany. The United States, and to a lesser extent Canada, are of the second kind. Canada may be seen as falling somewhere between the United States, on the one hand, and Germany and the rest of Europe on the other, having a regulatory environment somewhat more restricted than in the United States, but offering, at the same time, a wider variety of services than is likely to be available in Europe, at least in the short term.

In each of these countries, therefore, special considerations are relevant.

United States

- The widest variety of terminal equipment and network services is available here, but much of it is incompatible. Mixing and matching equipment from different suppliers, without relying on network conversions, may be difficult.

- Intelligent networks providing conversion between terminals will be widely available, reducing the problems created by the many terminal standards.

- Because standards will not be enforced within the United States, users who are likely to communicate internationally will have to take special precautions. Conversion services may be offered by international carriers, or by local carriers interconnecting with them, but the range and price of these services are not yet clear. Thus, equipment meeting international standards is preferable.

Germany

The German situation is extremely fluid in the wake of legal decisions restricting the Bundespost monopoly over terminal equipment. It seems likely that:

- A wide variety of competitive terminal equipment will become available.

- Since the Bundespost retains a monopoly on transmission, the variety of services, including intelligent networks, is likely to be limited.

- Communication with the rest of Europe is critical, and availability of conversion networks is uncertain. It is essential, therefore, that equipment conform to relevant CCITT standards, the most important of which is Teletex.

U.K. and France

- It seems likely that monopolistic attachment policies for terminal equipment will be liberalized. This is already underway in the U.K., where a telecommunications liberalization act was passed in 1981 (see Chapter 7).

- In France, Post Office monopolies on transmission are likely to limit the availability of intelligent networks.

- In the absence of intelligent networks, adherence of terminal equipment to a recognized standard, e.g., CCITT's Teletex, will be critical.

Canada

- Attachment policies will be more liberal than in France, for example, but less so than in the U.S.

- Intelligent network services should be widely available.

- Teletex will be offered, which will be of major significance for organizations contemplating text communications with Europe.

SUMMARY

We have discussed varied topics concerning electronic mail system design. Drawing on case studies, we have seen that:

- Multipurpose systems offer the opportunity to share the cost of electronic mail with other services.

- A trade-off exists between terminal cost and transmission speed which means for some message volumes, but not others, more expensive (faster) terminals are cost-effective.

- The optimum quality of display or printing also varies for different applications.

- Centralized and distributed systems both have advantages and disadvantages, depending on the application.

Further, we have examined the importance of privacy, security and compatibility.

In the next chapter, we will offer some guidelines on how to design an electronic mail system for your organization.

6

How To Design An Electronic Mail System For Your Organization

As we have seen, a properly designed electronic mail system must successfully balance a number of technological, economic and social factors in order to provide appropriate service. Deficiencies in even one area may cause a collection of elegant, high-technology hardware to provide far from satisfactory service, or to fall into disuse. Such imbalances may include:

- Terminal and transmission equipment poorly matched to the traffic placed on them;

- Terminal equipment of obsolete design, incapable of accommodating growth in electronic mail service;

- Management that fails to coordinate the novel demands of electronic mail;

- Staff who resist the introduction of electronic mail, or will not use it after its introduction.

This chapter summarizes a number of analytical and management techniques that will help to avoid these problems.

It should be recognized, of course, that a full and sudden transition to electronic mail will be made by few firms. This is because the infrastructure for full conversion — the terminal base, advanced transmission systems, etc. — does not yet exist. It is likely that organizations will begin by transferring part of their mail to electronic transmission and find that, as time goes on and the infrastructure develops, they can divert more and more items. The techniques described here are useful both for identifying what can be done prior to conversion, and for developing transition strategies.

ANALYZING YOUR BASIC REQUIREMENTS

At the outset, the following general considerations may guide organizations in analyzing their electronic mail requirements: intraorganizational requirements, organizational size and the importance of speed.

Intraorganizational Requirements

Electronic mail must be justified, initially, by its use for intraorganizational messages. A company simply cannot count on enough of its customers or suppliers having similar equipment — nor can it control the timing by which they install such equipment. There must be sufficient traffic within one organization itself to make feasible an electronic mail system.

Size of the Organization

Large organizations with many departments or many locations are the most logical users of electronic mail. The small or medium-sized company whose operations all take place under one roof typically won't be able to justify electronic mail. (Such a company may get electronic mail as a byproduct of a data processing or word processing system, or because it installs a modern records management/file retrieval system. It will not, with rare exceptions, find it economical to install electronic mail for its own sake.)

Importance of Speed

Organizations whose communications are particularly sensitive to speed are the best candidates for electronic mail. Of course, for every organization selling any good or service, receiving and catering to incoming orders demands fast processing. So does sending urgent messages to salespeople or customers. But for certain organizations, the provision of speedy transactions is the very essence of their service. Examples are travel agents or airlines who must confirm a booking immediately; banks that must transmit funds the same day; newspapers or broadcasters who must report the news as it happens. For these organizations, it is the usual message, not the unusual one, that requires speed and accuracy in handling.

SURVEY TECHNIQUES FOR DETERMINING MAIL FLOWS

Critical to a proper selection of equipment is a thorough knowledge of your organization's current mailflow. You can determine this by conducting the same kinds of mail surveys that have proven successful for measuring an organization's potential for conversion to electronic mail. Here again, the important variables are volume and the general characteristics of items sent.

Volume of Mail

Total current mail volume, with a reasonable allowance for growth, sets an upward bound on the capacity required by an electronic mail system. If a system has too low a capacity, significant traffic will continue to be transmitted by conventional means, and a portion of the potential benefit is squandered. In addition, overloaded systems are characterized by serious service problems: labor is wasted by queueing up to use terminals and messages are delayed by busy circuits or overloaded printers. On the other hand, a system of too high capacity may provide excellent service, but will tie up capital which could better be used elsewhere.

The mail volume survey must be sensitive not only to the average volume of mail sent, but also to the normal variations in volume. Many organizations have one or more regular, and identifiable, traffic cycles of varying duration; for example, days at the end of each accounting or billing period will have many more items than others. In addition, seasonal businesses will have heavy traffic in some months, and light traffic in others. In this case, a system configured to handle average load in fact may not be able to handle the majority of traffic. Therefore, the survey period must cover peak traffic times. An annual total can either be estimated by disregarding a portion of the peak traffic for estimation purposes, or, preferably, by broadening the survey base to include off-peak times as well.

Total volume should be easy to measure. If mail is handled centrally, it can simply be counted at the mailroom. Otherwise a brief questionnaire can be distributed to all employees handling mail, asking them to report the number of items they sent out or received that day. Such a questionnaire is easy to fill out, and may be repeated as often as necessary to get a fair sample of the variation.

It is also useful to quantify the total expenditure on postage and special courier or messenger services. Particular attention should be given to the latter, since even a relatively few items sent by special services can make up a high proportion of total expenditure. This information can often be derived from normal bookkeeping, or can be requested on the survey form.

Characteristics of Mail Items

After establishing total mail volume and expenditure, it is essential to discover the characteristics of mail items. In general it is neither necessary nor desirable that an exhaustive survey of all items be taken. Description of a mail item, even on a precoded form, takes a significant amount of time, and response rates will be low if every item must be described. Instead, a sample can be constructed by giving each employee who handles mail a limited number of coding forms and asking him to describe a few of the items he sends out. (Say, the first item mailed in each three-hour period spread over a day.) Employees handling greater amounts of mail should be given a proportionally larger number of forms. A sample form is illustrated in Figure 6.1.

A number of mail characteristics are of interest in this survey.

Description of Contents

A general description of contents is critical to determining whether facsimile or text systems will be adequate and to establishing a realistic estimate from the total volume survey. Typewritten documents, or photocopied documents which were typed within the organization (so that the electronic form is accessible) are usually suitable for text transmission. Other kinds — printed, handwritten or other photocopies — are likely candidates for facsimile.

Bulky items — books, journals, merchandise, large pieces of paper, etc. — are unsuited to electronic transmission.

Size of Contents

This is, simply, the number of pages of information. A large number of multi-page items indicates that multi-page handling capability must be built into the system. It also allows estimation of electronic mail transmission cost.

Destination

Information about the destination is useful:

- If the addressee is intraorganizational, for estimating the traffic for private electronic mail systems;

- If the addressee is one to which there is a large volume of mail (even if external to the organization) particularly if the addressee has adopted or is planning to adopt electronic mail in some form;

- For estimating transmission costs, since this is often a function of distance.

Figure 6.1 Sample Mail Questionnaire

Mail Survey

Description of Mail Item

1. Please describe the contents of this mail item.
   You may circle more than one

   Handwritten letter .1
   Original typed letter 2
   Tables of numbers 3
   Copied or printed document
      (black and white) 4
   Printed document (colored) 5
   Graphs or diagrams 6
   Book/periodical 7

2. What size are the pages?
   You may circle more than one

   The same size as this sheet
      or smaller 1
   Larger than this sheet 2
   Twice as large as this sheet
      or larger 3

3. If the item contains photocopied pages, was the original typed within the organization?
   Circle one only

   yes/no

4. If this item of mail contains any **handwritten, typed** or **printed** documents, please indicate how many pages there are in total.
   Write in the number of pages

   Handwritten

   Typed/printed

5. Where is this item being sent?
   Circle one only

   Own organization .1
   Parent or subsidiary organization 2
   Other organization 3
   Address . . . .
   . . . .
   . . . .
   Private address 4

6. To approximately how many miles away will this item be sent?
   Circle one only

   Less than 10 miles (16Km) 1
   10-29 miles (16-47Km) 2
   30-99 miles (48-159Km) 3
   100-250 miles (160-400Km) 4
   More than 250 miles (400Km) 5
   International 6

7. Please indicate the method of sending this item.
   Circle one only

   First class mail. 1
   Second or third class 2
   Parcel post 3
   Express mail 4
   Other post office service 5
   Commercial delivery service 6
   Internal van or car service 7
   Messenger 8
   Other (please specify) 9

8. What is the cost of postage or messenger (if known)?
   Specify amount $

9. When do you require delivery of this item?
   Circle one only

   Within 2 hours 1
   Today 2
   Next working day .3
   Within the next 5 working days 4
   Later than 5 working days 5

Method of Sending

This information is critical in relating the sample back to the overall survey of mail volume. It may also reveal useful patterns within each mailing category. For example, a high proportion of items sent by courier might be typewritten letters, while most second-class items might be printed materials. Thus a limited-capacity text-only system would be able to displace the bulk of the most expensive traffic.

Of course, this questionnaire should be tailored to individual requirements. Some organizations, for example, may have only a single office themselves, but may have heavy correspondence with a few major customers who are equipped for electronic mail. In this case, rather than having an internal/external question, the survey form might carry a check-list for these major customers.

ANALYSIS OF SURVEY RESULTS

Analyzing the survey results can provide a wealth of information necessary for planning the electronic mail system best suited to an organization. The results should form the primary basis for developing a system specification, and for dealing with equipment suppliers and carriers.

Figure 6.2 illustrates a general format that can be used to organize the survey data. The basic process is to develop the proportion of items in the detailed sample which fall into the various slots listed on the form, and then to project these back to the total volume and expenditure survey.

For example, a text-only item is one that is either typewritten or photocopied from an internally typewritten original. All other items must be sent by facsimile. Of course, you must exercise judgment in analyzing these results: for example, it may be standard practice to include printed brochures with typewritten correspondence which does not necessarily require them. This would tend to bias the results away from text-only, and should be corrected.

COST/BENEFIT ANALYSIS

A completed analysis of this sort allows the next stage to begin: identification of the most likely traffic for displacement to electronic mail and the assessment of the cost and benefits. In the early 1980s, practically the only traffic for displacement will be intraorganizational, since general penetration of electronic mail terminals in the overall population will be low. However, hybrid

Figure 6.2 Electronic Mail Traffic Analysis Form

Delivery Requirement	Intraorganizational		Outside Organization	
	Text	Facsimile	Text	Facsimile
Two-hour				
Average volume				
Peak volume				
Average distance				
Current cost				
Same Day				
Average volume				
Peak volume				
Average distance				
Current cost				
Next Day				
Average volume				
Peak volume				
Average distance				
Current cost				
Other				
Average volume				
Peak volume				
Average distance				
Current cost				

services will be developing rapidly during the early 1980s, and their availability will affect the usefulness of electronic mail for external mail. Thus, an estimate of total displaced traffic might include a high proportion of intraorganizational traffic, and a low proportion of external items (which would rely largely on hybrid services).

In a similar manner, traffic that requires quick delivery is the most likely to be displaced initially. These items generally represent a disproportionately high expense, and, as we have seen, even without special transmission services electronic mail is cost-effective compared to conventional alternatives.

To judge the benefit of an electronic mail system, two factors must be considered. One is some valuation of the increased convenience which an electronic system would provide, and the value of any "generated traffic," i.e., correspondence that would not be sent out if the electronic system was not available. The other is the displaced cost of items which would ordinarily be sent by other means.

Generated Correspondence

In the category of generated correspondence are tables of information or letters which otherwise would be dictated over the telephone, or last-minute sketches which simply could not be sent by any other means. Thus, a considerable element of judgment must enter into this calculation.

However, there is also a risk that a system introduced to handle priority traffic (e.g., for items formerly sent by courier) may, if made too readily accessible, be used for other items which are more cheaply and adequately sent by conventional means. Thus the value of generated traffic can be negative if care is not taken in developing regulations for the system's use which are neither too liberal, nor so restrictive as to block legitimate use.

Cost Savings

The cost of an electronic mail system can be estimated using the bids received from suppliers. It should be noted that text systems will generally be a marginal cost over the price of word processing or data processing, which are already justified for other uses. Facsimile, on the other hand, will usually have to be fully costed. Transmission charges can be estimated from the number of items, their length, and the average distance they must travel. (As explained in Chapter 3, however, the charging structure of the transmission network can complicate this computation.)

The result of this analysis should be a number of system options of different capacity, cost and benefit. In the final analysis, the assessment of indirect benefit will often be the determining factor in choosing one system over another. For example, a limited system designed only to replace some portion of intraorganizational courier traffic might be justified strictly on the basis of direct financial benefit. A larger system might allow more routine traffic to be carried as well, but not be justified on the narrow financial grounds of direct cost savings. Nevertheless, one might decide to build such a system on the basis of its improvement of intraorganizational communications.

IDENTIFYING THE CRITICAL USES AND USERS OF ELECTRONIC MAIL

A quantitative mail survey which yields overall patterns of postal usage may be essential to consideration of electronic mail, but the person doing the analysis must also exercise judgment about what and who are most important to the organization. Perhaps this can be done by interviewing the heads of major departments within the organization, e.g., marketing, production, finance, or perhaps it can be done by having one or more top executives involved in the analysis. Such an analysis might result in a ranking of five or six applications for which electronic mail will either produce better results than existing communication channels, cut costs, or in certain cases, result in increased profits. For example, a diversified manufacturing company might come up with the following list:

User	Need	Type of message required
Financial vice president	Immediate investment decisions of company's excess cash	Brief; text only, to banks/brokers
General counsel	Immediate transmission of legal papers	Lengthy; text only, to and from outside counsel
Marketing department	Immediate receipt of customer orders	Brief; text only, from customers
Marketing department	Transmit customer RFPs to headquarters, and respond with detailed quotes	Brief and lengthy; text and exhibits, to and from sales reps
Production department	Supplies and spare parts orders	Brief; text only, to suppliers

Understanding where electronic mail can make a critical difference to an organization will also help in instituting it. Unless a company is going to move immediately to a centralized system of electronic mail, the need will be to set up priorities for using the terminals, to place terminals in the best location, and to train people in their use. All of these tasks will be more easily accomplished once a company has ranked the types of uses by importance to the company.

DECIDING NOT TO USE ELECTRONIC MAIL

One of the outcomes of a survey of mail usage may be not to use electronic mail. It may be that the volume of urgent messages is not as great as was thought, or that the type of traffic sent by courier — e.g., bulky reports, large-sized engineering drawings, replacement circuit boards — can't be transmitted over terminals. This is a perfectly reasonable conclusion, and no organization should feel pressured to adopt an electronic communication system simply because it has studied its feasibility. Whether or not the company goes ahead with this investment, the fact of doing a survey is bound to yield valuable insights into existing communication patterns. And one outcome might well be the shifting of message traffic among conventional vehicles — or preliminary steps toward electronic mail, like expanded use of telex, or acquisition of word processors that can communicate.

MAKING THE TRANSITION
TO ELECTRONIC MAIL

Assuming that the cost/benefit analysis results in the decision to introduce electronic mail, there are a number of elements outside of the analysis that must be considered. Among them are:

- system reliability, availability and quality of maintenance;

- reproduction quality of printers and displays under field conditions;

- ease of operation;

- employee acceptance;

- level of generated correspondence.

In addition there is the possibility that the initial survey was in error, and that the displaceable traffic is either higher or lower than expected, or that the cost of transmission was incorrectly estimated. One way to reduce these risks is to conduct a field trial before investing heavily in an electronic mail system. Obviously, the results of such a trial must be interpreted carefully, since the value of a full service will likely be higher than of a limited one. (Here again is the principle of a large network being more valuable than a small one.) Another way is to develop strategies both for dealing with vendors and for preparing the organization for change.

Dealing with Vendors

A major factor in dealing with vendors is the quality of service and maintenance they provide. But in addition, the marketplace during the 1980s will be extremely competitive and it is uncertain at this point which vendors will be successful and which equipment will be standardized. Thus, organizations which commit themselves too early to a particular system may find that the vendor goes out of the electronic mail business, or that the equipment becomes obsolete because it fails to conform to what becomes the general standard. Furthermore, many organizations may require substantial investment in word processing immediately, but cannot justify communication capability until the capacity for external communication is more fully developed.

Given these considerations two strategies are valuable for dealing with vendors: one is to lease equipment on short terms; the other, if purchase seems advisable, is to negotiate a modification agreement in advance. For example, many new word processors are being designed to allow communications to be added in a modular way. Negotiation of a formal agreement for such a modification ensures that the vendor selected will be supporting electronic mail applications for its word processing systems, and reduces the likelihood of an organization being left behind by advances in the marketplace.

Organizing Your Company for Change

Next, management must consider the impact of electronic mail on both the organization and the people who will be affected by it. Electronic mail places unique demands on the employees of any company which introduces it. It combines technical areas of expertise that are often managed by different people, and requires new job skills and the alteration of long-established patterns of working. These changes, if not accomplished smoothly, can mean the difference between the successful and unsuccessful application of electronic mail — even for systems which are technically perfect.

Who Should Manage?

Electronic mail requires skills and responsibilities that in most organizations are three distinct managerial areas: communications, data processing and secretarial/production. As we have seen, the efficient use of electronic mail often depends on combining the resources of all three areas.

Coordinating the functions

Where these managerial functions are separated, as they are in many organizations, their effective coordination will be difficult, and tensions are likely to arise. Each manager will have legitimate concerns, not all of which may be shared by the others. Each is used to an unfettered freedom of action within his area of responsibility. And each manager may have specialized skills in one area, but be ignorant of the problems in others.

Creating a new department

Most organizations will try to resolve these tensions by vesting responsibility for electronic mail with the manager of one or the other of the areas mentioned. The telecommunications manager is generally a technical expert on transmission networks and costs (although sometimes only with voice and analog ones), and has practical experience with such matters as wiring buildings and dealing with terminal vendors and carriers. The data processing manager, on the other hand, will have a great deal of technical knowledge of digital systems, and may be in the best position to integrate electronic mail and data processing as part of a wider office automation strategy. Neither the data processing manager, nor the telecommunications manager, however, will have a very detailed knowledge of the problems of managing secretarial services, of resolving pay and grading disputes that may develop, or of the problems of introducing a new technology into an established work-force — areas in which the office manager will be the expert. On the other hand, the office manager will often not have the technical expertise that either of the other two might provide, and will likely be the most conservative of the three.

These considerations illustrate that for some organizations a more radical reorganization may be called for: the combining of all three areas into a single department. The advantage of this is that the potential of all three areas in combination is made easier to exploit.

Achieving Staff Acceptance

Staff acceptance is a second critical area for management concern. Resistance may take several forms, each of which may be detrimental to the overall utility of a system.

Operator ergonomics

First, if the operator ergonomics are not well thought out, staff may prefer traditional methods over electronic mail, and less than the full proportion of traffic will be diverted. Many of these operator considerations were discussed in some detail in Chapter 2. Briefly, they include providing such features as:

- message entry independent of destination terminal being busy; i.e., store-and-forward;

- automatic multi-page handling;

- high quality visual displays.

Importance of existing work patterns

A more subtle consideration is whether the new devices are compatible with social or work patterns within the office. An electronic mail terminal located somewhere in a building may be much less convenient than an out-tray on the desk in which ordinary mail items can be placed. Alternatively, a local terminal may be noisy and interfere with the concentration of other workers in the area.

Involvement of staff in the planning process

An important means for reducing the likelihood of these problems arising is to involve the staff in the planning process. This has practical benefit both in the information which the staff can provide the management, and in the awareness and identification with the project that is created. The initial focus for this can be the mail survey discussed earlier. In later stages of planning, individual interviews and group discussions with key personnel who handle the mail will provide insight into the necessary design parameters of the system. Finally, staff reaction to specific proposals by the system designers and to field trials as they are conducted can often improve the design, and in addition reduce the likelihood of staff resistance to full implementation.

Management's awareness of staff concerns

Besides staff resistance to functional problems with an electronic mail system, however, there may be more active forms of resistance as well. As already noted, the introduction of a word processor may also signal the beginning of a typing pool, and this may not be welcomed by some employees. Similarly, many employees may feel threatened by the introduction of the new technology: some excellent typists have neither the desire nor the temperament to learn how to use a word processor, and staff may worry that the introduction of the new technology may eliminate their jobs altogether.

It is essential that management be sensitive to these concerns. It must, first of all, offer training programs to staff whose jobs are changing due to the introduction of electronic mail. At the same time management must be aware that some employees will not wish to retrain, and should look, whenever possible, to jobs in other areas of the organization where these employees' skills are needed.

An important consideration in this effort is, however, that electronic mail, by itself, will generally have little effect on overall amount of employment within a firm. (This, of course, may not be true of full office automation.) It will, of course, require new skills, but the emphasis of electronic mail is not to eliminate jobs — since most organizations presently rely on the postal service for mail carrying — but to allow the organization as a whole to operate more effectively.

SPECIAL NOTES TO TELEX USERS

Telex offers many users an entirely satisfactory and valuable service, and it has an important advantage for external communications in that it is a widely recognized standard with a large terminal population. Nevertheless, as has been repeatedly illustrated, telex offers only a very limited service compared to full possibilities of electronic mail.

Therefore, most current telex users will want to retain the capability for telex use, but be able to expand to broader electronic mail applications. Two options are immediately apparent:

- the adoption of communicating word processing equipment which can conform to the CCITT's Teletex standard;

- subscription to an intelligent network service, if this is available, which can convert between telex standard and the standard for the new text equipment.

In some countries, however, regulations may prohibit the connecting of a communicating word processor to the telex network and/or block the development of intelligent networks. These issues are explored more fully in Chapter 7.

SUMMARY

We have seen that the design of an electronic mail system involves a number of techniques. A survey of current mail flows is the critical first step, and must reveal not only average volumes but also peak volumes, physical characteristics of items and their delivery priority. With this as the starting point, management can then draw up system specifications and implement a cost/benefit analysis which will determine whether an organization can benefit from electronic mail.

We have noted the usefulness of field trials to reduce risks before committing heavily to an electronic mail system. Finally, we have presented a number of techniques for dealing with vendors, and for preparing the organization for making the transition to an electronic mail system.

Section III: Policy and Market Analysis

☑ **Policy and Regulation Issues in North America**

☑ **User Alternatives**

☑ **Policy and Regulation in Western Europe**

☑ **Consequences of Current Policy**

☑ **Who Will Offer Services**

☑ **Transmission Services in North America**

☑ **Transmission Services in Western Europe**

☑ **Growth of Electronic Mail in North America and Western Europe**

☑ **Conclusions**

7

Policy and Regulation Issues

As seen in the previous chapters, a fully effective electronic mail system depends on the availability of services and terminal equipment, not all of which may be available or, if available, whose installation may not be sanctioned by telecommunications carriers. These carriers are, within certain limits, publicly controlled: in North America, carriers are private companies which are heavily regulated by government; in Europe they are generally government departments or government-held corporations (known as PTTs).

Although the details differ from country to country, all carriers enjoy certain monopolistic or semi-monopolistic privileges under law. In return, they have the obligation to provide telecommunications services at a reasonable rate to users.

It is these monopolistic protections, however, which may retard the development of electronic mail. Carriers are huge organizations with wide ranges of services to provide. Particularly if monopoly protection is strong, as is the case in most Western European countries, carriers have few incentives to change, and many disincentives. Therefore, they may not wish to provide services which some users will find desirable, and they may attempt to block the provision of service by others to protect their monopoly. Carriers' policies are not immune, however, to action and persuasion by users.

On the other hand, lack of regulation can be an equally serious problem: competition can lead to service fragmentation among various carriers, increase costs and reduce the number of addressees who may be easily contacted.

In both of these cases, users have two weapons at their disposal:

- consumer actions, including lobbying, consumer organization and legal means;

- the pace and manner of their own adoption of electronic mail.

Since conditions in Western Europe and North America differ so greatly, it is useful to discuss their particulars separately.

NORTH AMERICA

United States

In the United States, and to a lesser extent in Canada, the problems of users are quite different from those in Europe. Since the early 1970s, the Federal Communications Commission (FCC) has tried to make business telecommunications more competitive and more responsive to marketplace forces. Terminal attachments policies are extremely liberal, value-added services are permitted, although carefully regulated, and a number of carriers compete with AT&T for all forms of transmission.

In the U.S., sweeping changes are underway in the telecommunications industry as a result of government action and technological advances. Because the complexion of the industry changes almost daily, it is impossible to give a fully up to date picture of these changes. However, some of the major policy issues include:

- Deregulation/reorganization of AT&T. In a decision that could virtually reorganize the telecommunications industry in the U.S., the Justice Department announced in January 1982 that it had arrived at a settlement with AT&T regarding its seven-year antitrust suit against the communications giant. Under the terms of the agreement, AT&T would divest itself of its 22 local operating phone companies, while retaining its long lines service, research and manufacturing facilities, and be free to enter the data processing field. AT&T's initial offering in this field will be Advanced Communications Service, a data transmission network on which it also plans to provide electronic mail service in late 1982. The proposed settlement comes on the heels of the Telecommunications Competition and Deregulation Act passed by the Senate in 1981, and scheduled for consideration by the House in early 1982. Any Congressional action will have to take into consideration the Justice Department settlement, although it is possible that Congress will alter some of the terms of that settlement.

- Increased competition in domestic and international record communications. Western Union's domestic telex monopoly no longer exists as Graphnet and others offer services. Western Union, in turn, is seeking to enter the international message communications field from which it was previously barred.

- Division of responsibilities between the FCC and state public utility commissions. Recent actions of the FCC and Congress regarding the breakup and deregulation of AT&T will affect the way state commissions set local phone rates.

- The speed of the introduction of competing telecommunications technologies. These range from microwave common carrier services to satellites to broadband cable television systems with two-way or switching features.

While the trend is clearly toward deregulation and competition, and while this favors the introduction of new services like electronic mail, the immediate future will be confused, with many competing services and a lack of clearcut jurisdictions. The FCC's battle with the U.S. Postal Service over E-COM (see Appendix A) is only one of the governmental disputes likely.

Lack of Standardization

Because there has been no single body in the United States coordinating terminal equipment, there are effectively no compatibility standards; emphasis has been on the provision of intelligent networks for translation between terminals. However, such networks carry a considerable overhead cost associated with translation and ultimately they cost more than a less sophisticated network—resulting in higher prices to users. Moreover, while competition is allowed between alternative networks, the interconnection between them is sometimes difficult, and certainly not standardized or even obvious to the user. This results in an effective fragmentation of the market, and opens the possibility that some electronic mail users will be inaccessible to others.

User Alternatives

Fortunately, however, users in the United States have a wide range of tools with which to affect these developments:

- The FCC and Congress are both sensitive to user needs and concerns.

- The availability of terminals and services is demand-driven to a certain extent, and will be increasingly so. Therefore, consumer action—either direct or indirect—can have an effect. For example, if enough consumers choose terminal equipment based on its adherence to an international standard, most manufacturers would be forced to follow suit.

- Legal review of common carrier policies and tariffs is effective, if cumbersome. For example, legal decisions were the original basis of the liberal policies which now exist with respect to terminal attachment.

Canada

In Canada, the competition between the telephone companies comprising the Trans Canada Telephone System (TCTS) and Canadian National/Canadian Pacific Telecommunications (CN/CP) has provided Canada with some of the most advanced transmission services in the world. This is increasingly true now that the Canada Radio-Television and Telecommunications Commission (CRTC) has ruled that the telephone companies of TCTS must allow interconnection between their networks and CN/CP's.

TCTS and CN/CP are regulated, however, by both the CRTC and provincial regulatory bodies. Their decisions can be overruled by the federal or provincial executive. Canadian users, therefore, should make sure that their views are represented at these levels.

WESTERN EUROPE

In Western Europe the PTTs play a critical role in advancing or retarding the development of communications markets. For the most part, they have strongly protected monopoly powers and can set the pace of market development by their procurement policies, by the type and quality of networks they provide, and by their policies concerning attachment and usage. For example, in the U.K., British Telecom (BT) (formerly the telecommunications division of the post office but now an independent corporation) generally has allowed only a limited number of standard terminal designs (which it markets and services) to be attached to the telex network. While this policy has had some advantages for users (for example, maintenance and spare parts are provided centrally) the BT-provided terminals tend to lag behind the state-of-the-art. Thus, most British Telecom terminals are noisy and bulky, while quiet and compact telex terminals have been on the market in North America for some time.

However, there is evidence that such policies are changing. Germany has a somewhat more liberal terminal attachments policy (but the Bundespost retains a strong monopoly over transmission). Perhaps the most dramatic policy changes have taken place in the U.K., where a deregulation bill (the British Telecommunications Act) was passed in 1981, breaking the British Telecom monopoly over equipment and transmission services. Private equipment manufacturers are gearing up to enter the subscriber equipment market, and at least one plan has been drawn up by an independent consortium to build a competing transmission network. While some confusion regarding equipment standards and international transmission rights will delay any immediate challenges, it is clear that the U.K.'s new liberalized telecommunications policy will have far-reaching effects in the near future.

Consequences of Current Policy

European telecommunications policies will become a more critical issue as communicating word processors become the installation of choice, and as the variations among terminal equipment become too great for the PTTs to handle alone. Then the absence of a liberal attachments policy will be a serious obstacle to full development of electronic mail. A similar obstacle would be the insistence of PTTs that their staffs maintain all terminals. This would mean that only approved designs which the staffs have been trained to service could be attached, and would be almost as serious an obstacle to full development as monopoly powers over attachment.

Other PTT decisions in the implementation of transmission systems could affect users. A critical one is the introduction of Teletex service (discussed in Chapter 5). The Bundespost (West German PTT) and Televerket (the PTT of Sweden) have committed to launching this service; other administrations have less developed plans. With Teletex likely to become the standard for electronic mail in Europe, countries that lag behind may find that their businesses are at a competitive disadvantage. Therefore, the rapid support of such a service is in the direct interests not only of the organizations that would or would not receive service, but also in the national interest.

Effects of Future Policy Decisions

Other possible actions by PTTs of concern to users include:

- Restriction of "value-added" services. An example of a value-added service is the translation between incompatible terminals. A private company might offer a transmission service using PTT lines, but using the company's own computer to do the conversion. Many PTTs construe such services as a violation of their monopoly, yet do not offer the service themselves.

- Attempts to limit the use of private wire networks by the adoption of usage sensitive pricing, in which charges are computed on the basis of the time a line is used, rather than on the basis of a flat fee. As noted in Chapter 5,

many companies find it cost-effective to lease dedicated private lines linking office locations where there is heavy telephone, data or electronic mail
traffic. Indeed, for most companies, the lines are justified by data and
voice traffic alone, even when this is well below 100% of the capacity of the
lines. Thus, intraorganizational electronic mail transmission will have zero
marginal cost for transmission, and this acts as a powerful inducement for
its introduction. Usage sensitive or volume-based pricing, however, would
damage the prospects of electronic mail by destroying the incentives for
fuller utilization of these private lines.

8

Who Will Offer Services

Subject to the regulatory considerations outlined in the previous chapter, it is likely that the 1980s will see a whole range of new telecommunications services being offered, some directed specifically at electronic mail, others not. Given the capital-intensive nature of telecommunications development, however, most of the services that will be available in the early 1980s must either be in the introductory phases now, or at least in the advanced planning stages. Thus, it is possible to predict with a fair degree of accuracy what services will be available by the early 1980s and who will be offering them.

Again, conditions will vary markedly between the United States and Canada on the one hand, and Western Europe on the other. Therefore we will examine each in turn.

TRANSMISSION SERVICES IN NORTH AMERICA

United States

Although dominated by AT&T and its subsidiaries, the U.S. telecommunications industry offers a wide range of different services and facilities from independent carriers—too wide a range to be covered fully here.

AT&T

The telephone network is highly developed with transmission rates of up to 4800 bps. In addition AT&T offers a number of switched or leased circuit data services:

- Dataphone-50: a 50k bps service, which will be made obsolete shortly by other services with lower prices.

- Dataphone Digital Service (DDS): a private line digital service for interstate point-to-point or point-to-multipoint service. Transmission rates up to 1.544 million bps are available.

- Advanced Communications Service (ACS): a data communications network service, first announced by AT&T in 1978, but delayed by various developmental problems. AT&T now expects to set up the service by mid-1982, and plans to offer customer equipment and services by 1983.

- In addition to ACS, in 1981 AT&T announced an interface that will enhance the existing telephone network by providing circuit-switched digital capability. This will enable users to transmit and receive digital data and analog voice transmissions over the telephone network. AT&T expects to be able to provide this capability by 1983-84.

Other Carriers

Transmission systems currently offered by companies other than AT&T include:

Graphnet: The Graphnet system

- permits any facsimile machine to communicate with any other;

- accommodates input from any digital device;

- converts computer output of documents to facsimile representation.

Its message services include:

- store-and-forward;

- multiple addressing;

- manual delivery by messenger or other means to locations not owning their own terminal.

ITT's Com-Pak Network: A similar system in some respects to Graphnet, Com-Pak offers an even fuller range of conversion services between incompatible terminals in addition to store-and-forward facilities.

GTE Telenet: A packet-switched network used mainly for terminal-to-computer use, but having the capability for terminal-to-terminal use. Currently, about 350-400 cities in the U.S. are being served, and there are connections overseas. The system is now compatible to the X.25 protocol* which should facilitate its interworking with other networks. Charges are distance-independent within the U.S., and are currently $1.00 per 1000 packets of (maximum) 128 characters transmitted.

In August 1980, Telenet introduced its Telemail electronic mail service, enabling users on the network to send messages back and forth, and to store text in the GTE Telenet computers. (See Appendix A for details.)

Tymnet: A packet-switching network operated by Tymshare, the computer time-sharing company. Tymnet has nodes in 250 cities in North America and overseas. Charges are competitive with those from Telenet. In 1978, Tymnet began offering its own electronic mail service, OnTyme. (See Appendix A for details.)

Satellite Business Systems (SBS): SBS (owned 42½% each by IBM and COMSAT, and 15% by Aetna Life and Casualty Corp.) provides large organizations with private line switched networks for integrated voice, data and image capability. The antennae for communication with the satellite are located on the customers' premises. A system including three earth stations, a network with high-speed data communications capability, video, voice transmission and electronic mail capability could cost $108,000 a month. Thus, its customers are very large companies with heavy interestablishment traffic. Service began in March 1981, with the launching of one satellite. A second satellite was launched in September 1981, which SBS expects will double its capacity by 1982.

Canada

The structure of telecommunications in Canada differs significantly from that in Western Europe or the U.S. There are two principal carrier groups: the telephone companies forming the Trans-Canada Telephone System (TCTS) and CNCP Telecommunications,** the former being the major providers of telephone service, and the latter providing message and data communication

---

*CCITT X.25 protocol is established as the primary international standard for packet-switched networks.

**A partnership of the telecommunications divisions of the Canadian National Railway Co. and Canadian Pacific Inc.

services. As the result of a recent regulatory decision however, it is possible to use the TCTS telephone network to interconnect with CNCP services. There is no independent carrier business in Canada, nonetheless a wide range of services is provided that parallels many of the independent offerings in the United States. For example, Canadian public data networks (PDNs) are more comparable to the network provided by Telenet than anything offered by AT&T.

Private Voice-grade Lines

Private voice-grade lines are available supporting, in some areas, up to 9600 bps transmission. Other services include Dataroute and Infodat, which are similar digital private line services offered by TCTS and CNCP respectively. They offer transmission speeds of up to 50,000 bps. Other private lines are available to the U.S., and to overseas countries via the international carrier Teleglobe Canada.

Switched Data Services

Switched data services include:

- *Multicom (TCTS)*: offers transmission of up to 4800 bps.

- *Broadband Exchange Service (CNCP)*: a network designed specifically for data transmission, it allows service at up to 48k bps.

- *Datapac (TCTS) and Infoswitch (CNCP)*: these are expected to be the principal data communications services in the future. They are packet-switched networks based on the CCITT X.25 protocol.

In addition, TCTS offers a Message Switching Data Service (MSDS)—a computer controlled store-and-forward message switching service for TWX and private line teletypewriter stations. While aimed at low speed terminals, the service offers a number of interesting facilities, including:

- speed and code conversion;

- multi-addressing;

- message retrieval (all messages are numbered by sending and receiving station, and "lost" messages may be retrieved until the end of the next business day);

- priority message service;

- error recognition.

Finally, not to be confused with the U.S. carrier of the same name, Telenet is a CNCP message-switched service essentially similar to MSDS, but telex-rather than TWX-based.

TRANSMISSION SERVICES IN WESTERN EUROPE

In Europe (unlike the United States where the total is less than 1%) some 7% to 10% of mail traffic is international. The single most important element in this traffic will be the increasing availability of Teletex. Initially this will be seen by many as a supplement to telex, but, as we have seen, the Teletex Standard offers a good basis for the implementation of a full-feature electronic mail service. The first country to receive Teletex service was West Germany, in 1981; Sweden expects to receive service by 1982. Other countries' plans are less definite, but it is unlikely that any of the major European authorities could afford to delay implementation of Teletex much beyond the mid-1980s.

The availability of domestic services applicable to electronic mail vary widely among European countries.

France

The telecommunications services in France lagged far behind those in other industrially developed countries until the end of the 1960s. Since then there has been a major capital investment program, to the point that the French PTT offers some of the most advanced telecommunications services of any European country—although overall system growth will still require some time to catch up.

The public telephone network permits data transmission up to 2400 bps. In addition, there are four advanced services:

Colisee

Colisee allows the automatic interconnection of PABXs (i.e., internal automatic telephone exchanges) serving different establishments of the same organization. Colisee is designed primarily for telephone traffic but data transmission at up to 2400 bps is also possible. Thus a Colisee user may well be able to avail himself of this system for intracompany electronic mail traffic, particularly for installing communicating text processors. Use of Colisee for overnight transmission can be very cost-effective, if all the fixed charges for Colisee are absorbed by its use for voice during the day.

Caducee

Caducee provides switched data transmission services at rates between 2400 and 9600 bps, or up to 72,000 bps for local connections. While it was developed primarily for computer data traffic, it is also useful for text transmission and digital facsimile.

Transpac

Transpac is the first European packet-switched network to use the CCITT X.25 protocol. It began service in 1978, and is planned to be available throughout France by 1985. While it has some of the disadvantages of electronic mail use discussed in Chapter 3 (limited packet-storing capacity, higher than necessary transmission speeds, etc.), its distance-independent tariffs may make it attractive to many users.

Transmic

This is a network of high speed leased data lines. Currently it is based on the analog telephone network, but plans call for conversion to digital circuits. Current transmission rates offered are 2400, 4800, 9600 and 48,000 bps. Eventually the digital network will be able to support speeds up to 2048 million bps. Transmic was originally designed for computer use, but may have some application for high-speed digital facsimile.

Federal Republic of Germany

The present networks in Germany are:

- the telephone network;
- telex and Datex network;
- network for fixed connections.

The telephone network is of very high quality and transmission rates of 9600 bps are generally possible.

The Bundespost set up the Datex network in 1967 for speeds of 50 to 200 bps using the switching and transmission facilities of the telex network (but not allowing interconnection between them). The Bundespost is now introducing electronic switching and new transmission systems to both networks, which will allow transmission of up to 48,000 bps. The general plan is to integrate both switching and transmission of data and text into one integrated network called IDN. A packet-switched service was introduced in 1980, conforming to the CCITT X.25 protocol.

Two message services were introduced in 1981. Telefax is a telephone network-based service for Group 2 facsimile equipment, allowing users to connect their own terminals and to be listed in both the telephone directory and a special directory as a facsimile user. Teletex, discussed earlier, also began service in 1981, using the IDN network for transmission.

United Kingdom

The keystone of future developments in the U.K. will be the introduction of System X, an integrated, fully digital transmission/switching system. The first exchanges will be installed by late 1981 or 1982, but it will not be until late in the decade that this will have a significant impact on electronic mail. It will take that long before a significant number of exchanges will be replaced by System X, and the strategy for their introduction makes digital data applications difficult until the network is virtually complete.

Data transmission over the telephone network is currently provided at up to 4800 bps, and via leased circuits to 48,000 bps.

The "midnight line" service currently offered is of considerable interest for electronic mail. It allows a subscriber to make unlimited use of his telephone for direct dialed calls between midnight and 6 a.m. for a flat fee. This service is ideally suited to an electronic message terminal equipped with storage and autodial facility. Compared to standard off-peak rates, midnight line service is cost-effective at volumes of 700 pages per month of facsimile or text. Of course, if the service is also used for data transmission, it becomes cost-effective even sooner.

Other European Countries

Denmark, Finland, Norway, Sweden

Denmark, Finland, Norway and Sweden jointly developed an integrated data transmission system called the Nordic Public Data Network. The primary function of the network is to provide switched data circuits and transmission rates between 600 and 9600 bps, but the intention is to eventually provide facilities for both packet- and message-switching as well. Full service (not including packet- or message-switching) was available in all four countries by 1980; a service date for packet- and message-switching has not been announced.

Belgium and Italy

In Belgium, the PTT is planning a circuit-switched digital data network to be implemented over the 1980s; a packet-switched system offering full service was implemented in 1980. In Italy, data transmission is being offered over the phone system at rates up to 4800 bps and over leased circuits at up to 48k bps, although service in most areas is much more limited. Starting in 1978, an integrated telex/data network was introduced, offering:

- abbreviated dialing;

- called and calling subscriber identification;

- multiple addressing.

Initial transmission rates were 50 to 300 bps. Future plans call for services to be available at 9600 bps in some areas.

Netherlands and Spain

In the Netherlands, a packet-switched network conforming to the X.25 protocol became operational in late 1980. Although designed primarily for large users, other subscribers may use the service as well. In the long term it is possible that circuit-switched systems will be made available in the 1980s. In Spain, a packet-switched network has been available since 1973, although it does not conform to the X.25 protocol. The Spanish PTT, Compania Telefonica Nacional de España (CTNE) also provides a service called Auxiliary Data Service, which is essentially a store-and-forward message service for terminal-to-terminal use.

Switzerland

In Switzerland, the PTT is currently implementing the first part of a circuit-switched data network. Six switching centers were operational by 1980. In 1978, an experimental public-switched message service with rates up to 9600 bps was introduced for access from the telex network and private telegraph lines. The facilities include:

- multiple and group addressing;

- "prioritized" service—i.e., call attempts every three or 15 minutes, for up to 12 hours until the call is completed;

- message storage and retrieval.

In addition, by the mid-1980s a digital voice and data network will be introduced, but will take up to 20 years to complete.

SUMMARY

In all of the countries cited, the basic infrastructure for electronic mail is being developed. Obviously, some countries are much further along than others. However, already in the United States and Canada, and increasingly in Europe, the transmission systems for extremely cost-effective and convenient electronic mail service are in place, and by the end of the 1980s this will be almost universally true.

9

The Growth of Electronic Mail

The previous chapters have covered the many factors that are coalescing in favor of the wide acceptance of electronic mail. These include the rapidly rising cost and deteriorating quality of traditional postal service, the continuing diffusion of word processing in offices based on its inherent advantages over conventional typing, and improving technologies of transmission, processing and display. Nevertheless, the question remains: "How big will electronic mail really be?"

There is of course no simple answer to this, since tremendous uncertainties exist in a number of important areas. The behavior of carriers, equipment manufacturers and regulatory bodies—of the business community, unions and the economy as a whole—all will have their impact.

In the course of their study, Mackintosh Consultants and Communications Studies and Planning Ltd. made various projections regarding the growth of electronic mail. These projections were based on market conditions in 1979. Of course, estimates made in 1981 would differ in several areas. For example, the growth in use of word processors (though not necessarily communicating word processors) is progressing at a much faster pace than originally expected; the introduction of Teletex is behind schedule in many countries; and the facsimile market is growing more slowly than forecast. However, the projections presented here remain useful in forecasting growth in this dynamic area.

NORTH AMERICA

In the United States, the installed base of electronic mail terminals will grow from under 200,000 in 1978 to over 1.1 million in 1987. The Canadian-installed base will grow from 1,100 to over 100,000 in the same period. These projections exclude telex, TWX and private-wire networks. Text will overtake facsimile as the terminal with the largest installed base only toward the end of the projection period, reflecting the considerably higher penetration of con-

119

ventional facsimile terminals in the United States compared to Europe. However, the combined text-and-graphics terminal will be the fastest growing terminal type, beginning early in the projection period.

Electronic mail traffic will reach 26 million items per day, with about 5% of all letter mail and about 20% of primary business-to-business mail included in that total. At the end of the projection period, growth will continue at about 21% per year in the United States and about 28% per year in Canada.

The value of terminal shipments in North America will be $1.6 billion per annum by 1987, compared to an estimated $700 million in 1982. The Canadian market will amount to about 10% of the U.S. market in value. Text terminals will show only moderate growth largely owing to a drop of greater than 50% in average unit prices. By 1987, about 300,000 terminals will be shipped each year in North America.

WESTERN EUROPE

The installed terminal base for Western Europe (not including telex and private-wire printers) is projected to increase 20-fold over the forecast period, from less than 40,000 in 1978 to almost 800,000 in 1987. The largest installed base will be for text terminals (enhanced telex and communicating word processors) with 55% of the total, while the fastest growth will be among combined text-and-graphics terminals—at about 49% per annum.

Total electronic mail is projected to reach almost 19 million items per day by 1987. This is equivalent to a diversion of over 5% of all conventional letter mail, and 10% of primary business-to-business mail. At the end of the projection period, electronic mail traffic will still be growing at a rate of 27% per annum.

Finally, by 1987 the electronic mail terminal market in Europe will be worth more than $1 billion (constant 1978), compared to only $80 million in 1978. As early as 1982, the forecast calls for a $400 million market. This represents nearly 250,000 terminals being shipped each year.

CONCLUSIONS

Any forecasts about growth of electronic mail are necessarily speculative. Moreover, they do not provide any specific guidelines for companies evaluating their own choices. Nevertheless, the forecasts do offer a broad gauge of the environment for electronic mail—and in so doing, they confirm the viewpoint conveyed elsewhere in this report. Electronic mail is ripe for development for at least four reasons:

- the cost of conventional postal services, and other delivery choices, continues to escalate, while service, at best, remains disappointing;

- the technology of microelectronics and telecommunications is advancing at a rapid enough rate to bring down the cost of storing and sending messages electronically every year;

- large organizations around the world are installing equipment and systems that create the infrastructure for electronic mail, from microcomputers and word processors to facsimile machines, leased lines and satellite earth stations;

- potential suppliers of electronic mail systems include some of the world's largest and most profitable companies, among them IBM, Xerox, Philips and Matsushita. By dint of their enormous expenditures on research and development, manufacturing and marketing, they are determined to create a market for automated office systems, including electronic mail (see Appendix A for a short guide to manufacturers and telecommunications suppliers).

As has been pointed out in this report, it will take quite a while before organizations can send electronic messages to and from other companies, because of the problems of incompatible equipment and lack of national or international standards. Thus, for the forseeable future, investment in electronic mail must be justified by improved results or lower costs for *internal,* not external, communications. But the organizations which act today to begin putting in place the elements of a modern electronic message system will be that much farther ahead when the broader uses of electronic mail start to blossom.

Appendix A: A Short Guide to Electronic Mail Suppliers

WHO WILL SUPPLY EQUIPMENT

Organizations that wish to adopt electronic mail will be able to buy equipment from several kinds of businesses, depending on the regulatory environment in their country and their preferences: directly from the equipment manufacturer; from the PTT or carrier; or from companies that package, assemble or modify equipment from other manufacturers.

In some countries, of course, there may be no choice but to buy the equipment which the PTT provides, or at least has approved for connection to the network. In other countries, such as the United States, the carrier itself is unlikely to provide any but the simplest range of terminals, and most will be purchased from other sorts of groups. It is likely, however, that as electronic mail develops, demand for terminals will outstrip the ability of the PTTs to supply them, and attachment policies will be liberalized.

CHOOSING A SUPPLIER

The choice of terminal equipment, therefore, will be within the control of the user. His decision on which equipment to buy, and from what kind of organization, should depend on a number of considerations including: performance of the equipment; ability of the vendor to service it; and the long-term support of the manufacturer.

Vendors will differ widely in their knowledge of customer requirements, and their ability to assist a user in designing an appropriate system. Some manufacturers eventually will be able to offer a "systems approach," a full range of compatible equipment from stand-alone word processors to computers and telephone exchanges, while others may only be able to sell small pieces of an overall system. Systems houses can fill the gap between these extremes, putting together complete systems from many different manufacturers' products.

PROBLEMS OF DEALING WITH SUPPLIERS

A serious problem with the current electronic mail marketplace is that no manufacturer, even the largest, markets complete electronic mail systems. Some can offer communicating word processors, some facsimile, others market order-entry or other data processing systems, but none offers the complete range. However, it is likely that as the concepts of electronic mail and office automation continue to gain acceptance, these marketing problems will be solved. In the meantime, organizations that wish to pioneer these concepts will find their task more difficult.

Because of the lack of integrated electronic mail offerings, customers are often forced to deal with two or three suppliers if they want to install a functioning service. The choices are almost bewildering: buy word processing equipment with communications features (including appropriate software) and arrange for telecommunications lines; buy packaged software for filing and sending messages that can be used with existing microcomputers; wait for established common carriers to offer electronic mail services including equipment rental; use the packet-switched networks available from specialized carriers; or some combination of the above. Since electronic mail has the aspects of both the office equipment market and the telecommunications service market, there is potential for competition between very different types of companies—as well as for confusion and frustration on the part of users. Users must be prepared for this state of affairs. They can buy an office typewriter with one phone call; they can order a new phone line with another call. No such simple one-step transaction will put in place an electronic mail system, however.

The manufacturers most likely to dominate the electronic mail market, at least throughout the early 1980s, probably are going to be the major multinational firms already in the office equipment field. Brief profiles given below illustrate the range of suppliers to the electronic mail market, and include descriptions of the relevant products or services offered by several firms in each category.

EQUIPMENT AND SOFTWARE SUPPLIERS

Apple Computer, Inc.

Apple is a leading manufacturer of microcomputers. In August 1981 Apple (and Microcom, Inc. of Boston, MA) introduced two software packages of interest to electronic mail users:

Micro-Courier: provides for overnight or instant transmission of messages, graphs, etc., from one Apple II microcomputer to another over standard telephone lines. In addition, messages can also be sent to a time-share data base or to a minicomputer, locally or nationwide. The package costs $250.

Micro-Telegram: also for use on Apple II microcomputers, this program allows access to Western Union communications lines. Users can send TWX, telex and international telex messages. This package also costs $250.

Digital Equipment Corp. (DEC)

DEC is a major manufacturer of small, medium and large-scale computer systems, as well as word processing equipment. In October 1981 it announced its Office Plus office automation program, along with the following product of interest:

DECmail: this software product supports full electronic mail service, and is designed to run on the DEC VAX 11 series minicomputers. DECmail provides electronic mail service and electronic file maintenance to existing data processing systems. The fully supported software (including training, warranty, etc.) costs $20,000; the software license alone sells for $12,000.

IBM

IBM already markets communicating word processors and has a very comprehensive product capability for the electronic mail market, currently lacking only facsimile machines. In addition, the company is presently showing considerable interest in the standards for Teletex. Two products of interest marketed by IBM's Office Products Division are:

IBM 6670 Information Distributor: a communicating word processor that combines electronic communications, laser printing for both word and data processing applications, text processing and copying. It is available through lease or rental plans, or for purchase at a cost of $75,000.

IBM Displaywriter: this is a multi-function, modular text processing system, introduced in June 1980. Licensed programs enable the system to perform mathematical functions, electronic file maintenance and records processing, and provide for an electronic dictionary function. Programming is available to support communication between the Displaywriter and various host IBM computers. A basic system sells for about $7900 and leases for $275 a month, not including licensed programs.

Sony Corp.

Sony Office Products division introduced the following products in 1981:

Series 35 word processing system: consists of a base work station, display unit and a high-speed printer. It is a lightweight modular unit, and uses microcassettes from other Sony dictation equipment, including the Typecorder (described below). Microfloppy disk drives are built into the keyboard. The basic unit (including printer and dual disk drives) starts at approximately $9000.

Typecorder: a portable electronic typewriter, weighing three pounds, with a built-in microcassette. The unit will take voice and text on the same microcassette, has text editing, dictation and transcription capability, and will communicate with a local or remote printer. Prices for the basic unit start at about $1450.

Wang Laboratories, Inc.

Wang is a major manufacturer of data and word processing equipment, small business computers and integrated information systems. It offers several products of interest:

Wangwriter: a stand–alone, communicating word processor with advanced text-editing capabilities. The unit has both data and word processing capabilities, and is compatible with all other Wang Office Systems products. The Wangwriter was originally priced at $7500, but was reduced to $6400 in June 1981.

Mailway: introduced in June 1979, Mailway is a software package (available on Wang word processing systems) that provides three levels of electronic mail options. Level 1 software allows communications from workstation to workstation over dial-up telephone lines, and costs $200 per system. Level 2 uses the Mailway Distribution Controller (MDC) unit as the distribution center and provides centralized control and automated mail collection and delivery. Level 2 software starts at $5000. Level 3 provides electronic mail capabilities and distributed data processing by using a Wang computer as the distribution center. Level 3 software starts at $9000.

WangNet: this is a local area communications network that uses coaxial cable to integrate electronic office equipment. It is a competing service with Ethernet (described below) and can link other manufacturers' equipment in addition to Wang products. WangNet is a broadband network which (unlike baseband networks such as Ethernet) can carry radio frequency transmission up to 50 miles. The service was introduced in June 1981, and test systems were being installed in December 1981.

Xerox

Xerox is the leading worldwide supplier of copiers and a major supplier of office equipment. Xerox has a ubiquitous sales and service organization, and has comprehensive in-house capabilities in many peripheral products relevant to electronic mail. Among the many new products introduced by the Xerox Office Products and Xerox Business Systems divisions, several are of interest:

Xerox 820 information processor: introduced in 1981, this is a desktop workstation that can be used as a word processor, desktop computer, or both. The computer version (including display screen, keyboard and disk storage) is $2995; the word processing version (with the optional printer) is $5895.

Xerox 8010 Star information system: also introduced in 1981, this is an executive workstation for professionals that has filing, text-editing and graphics capabilities. In addition to other functions, the system allows users to send electronic mail and print documents. It is compatible with the Xerox Ethernet local area network (see below). The basic system (including display, keyboard, control device and basic software) costs $16,595, or can be rented monthly for $695.

Ethernet: this is a local area baseband communications network introduced by Xerox in December 1979, and supported by Intel Corp. and Digital Equipment Corp. It is an office communications network that features high-speed data transmission rates, and uses coaxial cable and packet-switching of messages to link office equipment within an office and between offices in the same building. Xerox has brought out a line of office equipment based on Ethernet (such as the Star information processing system described above), however the network is designed to link equipment from other manufacturers as well.

One of the guiding principles behind Ethernet is Xerox's contention, based on research it has done, that most messages originating in an office go to a recipient within 100 yards of the person sending the message. This concept of electronic mail, while different from that used in this book (which concentrates on intraorganizational communication between different geographic locations) is nonetheless important to understand and deal with.

Other Equipment Suppliers

Dozens of other manufacturers around the world have entered the word processing equipment market, and in an increasing number of cases, they are offering machines that communicate over telecommunications networks. In the U.S., many mainframe and minicomputer manufacturers have moved into this field, among them Honeywell and Burroughs. In Europe, IBM has a leading position in word processing but Philips and Olivetti are strong contenders.

Although the Japanese manufacturers are relative latecomers to word processing, they are likely to devote increasing resources to this field. Already the Japanese dominate the worldwide market for facsimile transceivers; leading suppliers include Matsushita, NEC and Ricoh. Appendix B lists representative suppliers and their addresses.

SERVICE SUPPLIERS

Telemail (GTE Telenet)

Introduced in August 1980, Telemail is an electronic mail service operating on the Telenet network. Telemail customers pay a $140 per month subscription fee, as well as $14 per hour during business hours, dropping to $7 between 6 p.m. and 9 p.m., and to $4 at night. Storing 20,000 characters costs five cents per day.

OnTyme (Tymnet, Inc.)

OnTyme is an electronic mail service originally introduced in 1978. The service permits messages to be sent and received over the Tymnet network (just as Telemail operates over the Telenet network), and provides online file storage for messages. The newest version, OnTyme II, was introduced in March 1980. OnTyme II offers direct communication from ASCII terminals to facsimile terminals for hard copy output, and has an "electronic mailbox" feature. The average cost of preparing and sending a message is $.50. Average message lengths range from 500 to 1000 characters. OnTyme II is available anywhere in the U.S. on the Tymnet public packet network. Local call access is available from about 250 cities.

E-COM (U.S. Postal Service)

E-COM (for Electronic Computer Originated Mail) is the controversial electronic mail service offered by the U.S. Postal Service. The service began on January 4, 1982. E-COM allows the electronic transmission of bulk messages to 25 post offices around the U.S. Once received, the messages are printed out, automatically put into envelopes and delivered as regular mail. The system promises delivery of mail anywhere in the country within two days. Transmission services are leased or purchased from five carriers: TRT Communications, ITT World Communications, Netword, Taipan Industries and Dialcom, Inc. The service is geared toward high volume mailers who already employ computers to originate letters. At present, E-COM rates are 26 cents per first printed page and 10 cents per second printed page (there is a two-page limit to messages).

Much of the controversy surrounding E-COM has been over the regulatory issue regarding which agency has jurisdiction over the service, and the related political issue of allowing a government monopoly to enter the electronic mail field. Private companies fear that Postal Service entry into electronic mail will harm their own chances in this market.

Several government agencies have been involved in the dispute over E-COM. The Postal Rate Commission (PRC) opposed initiation of the service, and recommended instead a two-year experimental version of E-COM. However, the U.S. Postal Service sued the PRC and overturned this decision in May 1981. The Justice and Commerce Departments have also opposed the Postal Service's entry into electronic mail; one week before E-COM service was scheduled to begin, the Justice Department filed suit to have start-up delayed. Although this suit was unsuccessful, the Justice Department plans to continue its action.

These actions, combined with the concerns voiced by private companies, make the future of E-COM somewhat uncertain.

INTELPOST (U.S. Postal Service)

INTELPOST (for International Electronic Post) is an international digital facsimile network that transmits messages via satellite and uses existing postal delivery services for mail collection and distribution. The service, which was first introduced in the U.S. in 1980, offers same day or overnight mail delivery between the U.S. and other countries.

For regular service, the original document is scanned by a facsimile reader at the INTELPOST transmitting facility and sent via satellite (Intelsat IV-A). A facsimile printer at the receiving end prints the document, which is then placed in an envelope and delivered by postal personnel the next day. Several other modes of delivery are available at additional charges: special delivery, window pick-up and express mail. A black and white copy of any information that can be reduced to a maximum size of 8½x14 inches can be sent for a charge of $5.00 per page.

INTELPOST service is currently available between the United States (from New York and Washington) and all of Canada, the United Kingdom, Amsterdam and Buenos Aires. Service to Belgium, West Germany, France and Switzerland is expected to begin in 1982.

Appendix B: Directory of Suppliers

UNITED STATES

A.B. Dick Co.
5700 West Touhy Ave.
Chicago, IL 60648
(312) 763-1900

AMDAX Corp.
160 Wilbur Place
Bohemia, NY 11716
(516) 567-7887

American Telephone & Telegraph
195 Broadway
New York, NY 10007
(212) 393-9800

Apple Computer, Inc.
10260 Bandley Dr.
Cupertino, CA 95014
(408) 996-1010

Burroughs Corp.
Burroughs Place
Detroit, MI 48232
(313) 972-7000

Comptek Research, Inc.
Office Automation Division
One Technology Center
45 Oak St.
Buffalo, NY 14203
(716) 842-2700

COMPUCORP
1901 South Bundy Dr.
Los Angeles, CA 90025
(213) 820-2503

Compuserve, Inc.
5000 Arlington Center Blvd.
Columbus, OH 43220
(614) 457-8600

CPT Corp.
8100 Mitchell Rd.
PO Box 295
Minneapolis, MN 55440
(612) 936-8000

Cylix Communications Network
855 Ridge Lake Blvd.
Memphis, TN 38119
(901) 761-1177

Data General
Information Systems Division
4400 Computer Dr.
Westboro, MA 01581
(617) 366-8911

Datapoint Corp.
9725 Datapoint Dr.
San Antonio, TX 78284
(512) 699-7000

Digital Equipment Corp.
129 Parker St.
Maynard, MA 01754
(617) 493-2046

Exxon Office Systems
8 Sparks Ave.
Pelham, NY 10803
(800) 327-6666;
In Florida 1-800-432-0800

General Electric Information
Services, Inc.
401 North Washington St.
Rockville, MD 20850
(301) 340-4000

Graphic Scanning Corp.
329 Alfred Ave.
Teaneck, NJ 07666
(201) 837-5100

GTE Telenet Communications Corp.
8330 Old Courthouse Rd.
Vienna, VA 22180
(703) 827-9200

Hendrix Inc.
670 N. Commercial St.
Manchester, NH 03101
(603) 669-9050

Honeywell
200 Smith St.
Waltham, MA 02154

IBM Corp.
Parsons Pond Dr.
Franklin Lakes, NY 07417
(201) 848-2326

ITT Business Communications
10 E. 40th St.
New York, NY 10017
(212) 532-4700

Lanier Business Products, Inc.
1700 Chantilly Dr., N.E.
Atlanta, GA 30324
(404) 329-8000

Lexitron Corp.
1840 DeHaviland Dr.
Thousand Oaks, CA 91359
(805) 499-5911

Lexor Corp.
7100 Hayvenhurst Ave.
Van Nuys, CA 91406
(213) 786-1600

MCI Telecommunications Corp.
1133 19th St. N.W.
Washington, DC 20036
(202) 872-1600

NBI, Inc.
1695 38th St.
Boulder, CO 80301
(303) 444-5710

NCR Corp.
1700 S. Patterson Blvd.
Dayton, OH 45479
(513) 445-5000

NEC Information Systems, Inc.
5 Militia Dr.
Lexington, MA 02173
(617) 862-3120

Nixdorf Computer Corp.
168 Middlesex Turnpike
Burlington, MA 01803
(617) 273-0480

Northern Telecom, Inc.
Data Park
Minnetonka, MN 55343
(612) 932-8314

Olivetti OPE
505 White Plains Rd.
Tarrytown, NY 10591
(914) 631-3000

Philips Information Systems Inc.
4040 McEwen
Dallas, TX 75234
(214) 386-5580

RCA Global Communications
60 Broad St.
New York, NY 10004
(212) 248-2121

Satellite Business Systems, Inc.
8283 Greensboro Dr.
McLean, VA 22102
(703) 442-5000

Sony Corp. of America
9 West 57th St.
New York, NY 10019
(212) 371-5800

Source Telecomputing Corp.
(subs. of The Reader's Digest
Association, Inc.)
1616 Anderson Rd.
McLean, VA 22102
(703) 734-7500

Sperry-Univac, Inc.
17900 Von Karman Ave.
Irvine, CA 92714
(714) 557-9398

Tymnet, Inc.
20665 Valley Green Dr.
Cupertino, CA 95014
(408) 446-7000

U.S. Postal Service
Washington, DC 20260
(202) 245-4000

United Telecommunications, Inc.
PO Box 11315
Kansas City, MO 64112
(913) 676-3343

Vector Graphic, Inc.
500 North Ventu Park Rd.
Thousand Oaks, CA 91320
(213) 991-2302

Wang Laboratories Inc.
One Industrial Ave.
Lowell, MA 01851
(617) 459-5000

Western Union Corp.
1 Lake St.
Upper Saddle River, NJ 07458
(201) 825-5000

Western Union International
1 WUI Plaza
New York, NY 10003
(212) 363-6400

Xerox Corp.
Office Systems Division
1341 West Mockingbird Lane
Dallas, TX 75247
(214) 689-6000

FEDERAL REPUBLIC OF GERMANY

Nixdorf Computer AG
Fürstenallee 7
4790 Paderborn
200375

Olympia Werke AG
Postfach 960
2940 Wilhelmshaven
78 45 38

Siemens AG
Wittelsbacher Platz 2
D-8000 Munich 2

Triumph Adler Vertriebs-GmbH
Postfach 4955
D-8500 Nürnberg

FRANCE

CII-Honeywell Bull
94 Avenue Gambetta
75960 Paris Cedex 20
355-4433

CIT-Alcatel
10 bis rue Louis Lormand
F-78320 La Verriere

Secré
214-216 Faubourg
Saint-Martin
Paris (10e)

Thomson-CSF
173 Boulevard Haussmann
75360 Paris Cedex 08
256-96-00

ITALY

Ing. C. Olivetti & Co., S.p.A.
10015 Ivrea (TO)
Via G. Jervis, 77
(0125) 525

NETHERLANDS

Philips Data Systems B.V.
7300 AE Apeldoorn,
055 330123

UNITED KINGDOM

ITT Business Systems
Crowhurst Rd.
Hollingbury
Brighton
East Sussex

Plessey Communications
& Data Systems Ltd.
Beeston,
Nottingham
NG9 1LA
(0602) 254831

Nexos Ltd.
Nexos House
Whitefriars
Lewins Mead
Bristol

Rank Xerox Ltd.
Rank Xerox House
338 Euston Rd.
London, NW1 3BH
01-387-1244

TELECOMMUNICATIONS ADMINISTRATIONS

Fernmeldetechnishes Zentralamt
Arsenal
1030 Wien
Austria

Regie des Telegraphes et des Telephones
Service Transmission de donnees
Tour RTT — 17eme etage
Boulevard Emile Jacqmain, 164
B-1000 Bruxelles,
Belgium

Generaldirektoratet for P&T
Telestyrelsen
Farvergade 17
Dk — 1007 Copenhagen K
Denmark

British Telecom
OLC3.1
Broad St. South
55 Old Broad St.
London
EC2M 1RX
England

General Direction of Posts and
Telecommunications
Foreign Division
Box 528
SF-00101 Helsinki 10
Finland

Direction Generale
Direction des Affaires Commerciales et
Telematiques
20 rue Las Cases
75007 Paris
France

The Hellenic Telecommunications
Organisation
Customer Relations Department
Telex and Data Transmission Division
5 Stadiou St.
Athens 125
Greece

Telegraph Section
Department of Posts and Telegraphs
Marlborough St.
Dublin 1
Ireland

SIP D.R. Lazio
Via Usodimare, 32
Roma
Italy

Nippon Telegraph and Telephone
1-1-6, Uchisaiwai-Cho
Chiyoda-Ka
Tokyo, 100
Japan

Administration des P et T
Division Technique
S.A.T.
17 rue de Hollerich
Boite postale No. 2061
Luxembourg

Centrale Directie PTT
Centrale Afdeling Abonneezaken
Telecommunicatie
Postbus 30000
2500 GC The Hague
Netherlands

Oslo Teleomrade
Oslo 1
Norway

Reparticao de recepcao e apoio a
clientes especiais
Ra do Conde Redondo No. 79-50
1192 — Lisbon — CODEX
Portugal

Direccion General de Correos y
Telecomunicacion
Conde Penalver, 19
Madrid (6)
Spain

Central Administration of
Telecommunications,
Marketing Department
Data Communication
S-123 86 Farsta
Sweden

PTT General Directorate
Telecommunications
Coordinating Office Data
Communication
Vikoriastr. 21
CH-3030 Berne
Switzerland

Fernmeldetechnisches Zentralamt
Referat Datel Services
PO Box 5000
D-6100 Darmstadt
West Germany

Index

Other Titles from Knowledge Industry Publications

The Word Processing Handbook: A Step-by-Step Guide to Automating Your Office
by Katherine Aschner
191 pages

	hardcover	$32.95
	softcover	$22.95

Office Automation: A Glossary and Guide
edited by Nancy MacLellan Edwards
300 pages (approx.)   hardcover $59.50

Electronic Mail Executives Directory
compiled by International Resource Development Inc.
200 pages (approx.)   hardcover $120.00

Electronic Document Delivery: The Artemis Concept
by Adrian Norman
226 pages   hardcover $45.00

The Executive's Guide to TV and Radio Appearances
by Michael Bland
138 pages   hardcover $14.95

Managing the Corporate Media Center
by Eugene Marlow
215 pages   hardcover $24.95

The Future of Videotext
by Efrem Sigel, et al.
192 pages (approx.)   hardcover $32.95

Video Discs: The Technology, the Applications and the Future
by Efrem Sigel, Mark Schubin, Paul F. Merrill, et al.
183 pages   hardcover $29.95

Video in the 80s: Emerging Uses for Television in Business, Education, Medicine and Government
by Paula Dranov, Louise Moore and Adrienne Hickey
186 pages   hardcover $34.95

Available from Knowledge Industry Publications, Inc.,
701 Westchester Ave., White Plains, NY 10604